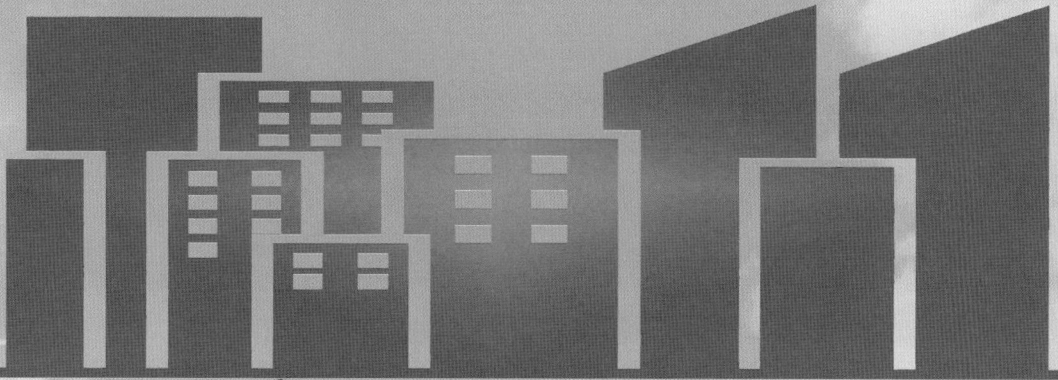

# Amazing Future Prospects

## —Exploring Human Activity—

## グローバル社会に生きる

### —聞く，読む，書く力を鍛える—

伊與田 洋之
赤塚 麻里
土居 峻
Marikit G. Manalang
室 淳子

NAN'UN-DO

Download Audio

**音声ファイル**
**無料 DL**
**のご案内**

このテキストの音声を無料で視聴（ストリーミング）・ダウンロードできます。自習用音声としてご活用ください。
以下のサイトにアクセスしてテキスト番号で検索してください。

**https://nanun-do.com**　テキスト番号［ **512219** ］

※ 無線 LAN（WiFi）に接続してのご利用を推奨いたします。

※ 音声ダウンロードは Zip ファイルでの提供になります。
　お使いの機器によっては別途ソフトウェア（アプリケーション）の導入が必要となります。

※ Amazing Future Prospects Exploring Human Activity
音声ダウンロードページは以下の QR コードからもご利用になれます。

*Read by*
Guy Perryman（英）
Jennifer Skidmore（米）

Amazing Future Prospects
—Exploring Human Activity—



by
伊與田 洋之／赤塚 麻里／土居 峻／ Marikit G. Manalang ／室 淳子

# はしがき

コロナウイルスの蔓延やウクライナ情勢などで世界は劇的に変化し，私たちは激動の時代の中で生きることを余儀なくされています。それと同時に様々な情報が世界を駆け巡り，遠隔地にいる人たちとのやり取りが容易になっていることを実感しています。グローバル化が確実に進んでいます。このことは，英語を主体とするコミュニケーション能力の重要性がますます高まっていることを意味しています。

このテキストは「インプットからアウトプットへ」をコンセプトにし，2019 年に出版した Amazing Visions of the Future の続編として，内容をグレードアップさせた中級編の総合教材として開発しました。執筆者が知恵を出し合い，学生の目線で，興味を持ちやすいトピックや内容を選ぶことを基本方針としました。リスニングとリーディングは TOEIC に準じた形式を取り入れ，試験対応を意識した内容にしています。ライティングでは，練習問題を拡充させ，リーディングで出てくる構文などを参考にして，表現力を向上させることを目標としています。

英語の学習者は自然な日常会話や英語のニュースなどを聞き取ったり，映画を字幕や吹き替えなしで楽しんだり，海外旅行で困らない英語力を身に付けたいと望んでいます。さらに一歩進んで，プレゼンテーション能力の向上や留学してコミュニケーション能力を飛躍的に伸ばしたいと考えている学習者も数多くいます。このテキストは中級者向けの教材として，より正確な読解や豊かな表現力が養えるよう配慮しています。

本書の特色は，豊富で多彩なトピックを取り上げ，学習者の興味・関心を引き付ける工夫をしていることです。さらには，各ユニットを構成するリスニング，リーディング，ライティングのセクションを有機的に関連させ，1 つのトピックをインプットからアウトプットへの流れの中で学習できるようにしています。リスニングセクションの最後のエクササイズはプレ・リーディング・アクティビティになっていて，リーディングへの橋渡しをしています。リーディングで内容を把握したあと，本文中の構文や言い回しを参考にして，ライティングできるようにしています。ライティング科目の教材としても活用できます。

異なる考え方や視点や持った執筆者が，それぞれのトピックを統一されたフォーマットで分かりやすい英文で解説しています。現代社会の問題点を提起しているトピックもあります。学習者に幅広い知識・知見・感性を与える機会を増やすことがねらいです。各セクションには，定着をはかるためにエクササイズを設けています。間違いを恐れずに果敢に挑戦してください。ただし，自分が間違えたところから学ぶ，という観点を忘れないでください。

英語学習を通して，教養を深めるとともに，外国人のものの考え方を理解し，自分の国の文化を発信できるようになることを願っています。

2024 年 4 月

執筆者一同

## 本書の構成

### *Listening*

英語の音声の聞き取りを助けるヒントを簡潔に紹介しています。語アクセント，文アクセントなどの基本的なルールから，消こえなくなる音，弱形と強形，つながる音，英語のリズムなど，英語の音声の特徴について解説しています。学習に入る前のウォーミングアップに役立ちます。

***Exercise 1*** 何についての説明かを聞き取り，それを日本語で答える問題です。一語一語にこだわるのではなく，全体として，内容を捉える練習です。

***Exercise 2*** 発話とそれに対する３つの応答を聞き，発話に対する最もふさわしい応答を１つ選ぶ問題です。TOEIC® L&R Test の Part II Question – Response に対応した問題です。

***Exercise 3*** Reading Passage のトピックに関連する Opening Conversation を聞き取り，会話の内容に関する質問に答える問題です。内容を聞き取ると同時に，Reading Passage への意識付けができます。

### *Reading*

各ユニットのトピックに関連した題材を取り上げた 330 語前後の英文です。色々な話題を英語で考えながら，その視野を広げられるように工夫しています。

***Exercise 1*** 多項選択式で本文の内容理解を確認する問題です。

***Exercise 2*** 本文の内容について真偽を問う問題です。

**トピック・コラム**

Reading Passage で取り上げたトピックに関連して，興味を起こさせるような情報を日本語で説明しています。トピックについてさらに知識を広げ，考察を深めるのに役立ちます。

### *Writing*

***Exercise 1*** 空所補充形式で，本文中に出てくる重要語句やフレーズを確認する問題です。

***Exercise 2*** 語句を並べ替えて英文を完成させる問題です。最初の設問のみ日本語訳でヒントを付けています。

***Exercise 3*** 本文で出てきた重要表現を参考にして，英文を書く問題です。

**付録**

音声学的観点から，強アクセントと弱アクセント，日本語と英語の違い，リズムなどを解説しています。英語らしい発音を意識し，特に，リスニング力やスピーキング力などの向上にも活用できます。また，Reading Passage を読むのに必要な語彙の一覧や文法項目を記載しています。

# Contents

# Unit 1

# College Education

## 大学の教養科目群

## Listening

### Warm Up

02

**◆ 語アクセント ◆**

日本語は高低のアクセントで発音されるのに対して，英語は強弱のアクセントで発音されます。強弱の付け方によって違う単語になることもあるので，注意が必要です。また，複合語も１つの単語として強弱アクセントが付きます。

1. **ad**dress 住所
2. ad**dress** 演説する
3. **green**house 温室
4. green **house** 緑の家
5. **white**board 白板
6. white **board** 白い板

**Exercise 1** 音声を聞いて，どんな科目の説明かその名前を日本語で（　　）内に書き入れましょう。 03

A（　　　　　　　　　）　B（　　　　　　　　　）　C（　　　　　　　　　）

**Exercise 2** 音声を聞いて，最も適切な応答を一つ選びましょう。 04

1. (A)　(B)　(C)　　2. (A)　(B)　(C)　　3. (A)　(B)　(C)　　4. (A)　(B)　(C)

**Exercise 3** Opening Conversation を聞いて，下の質問に答えましょう。 05

1. 雅は何を提案したのか。

______________________________

2. 中世のヨーロッパで学生が本をなかなか使えなかったのはなぜか。

______________________________

# Reading

▶ 英文を読んで質問に答えましょう。

06

Have you ever heard of Liberal Arts or General Education? Most universities require their students to take a set of such courses. The English class you are now taking might be one of them. But how did these courses come to be?

In America, where higher education does not have a long history, practical learning was the focus of education. Fields of study such as engineering, agriculture, business administration, and applied science were at the center of higher education. There was a need to provide basic knowledge serving as the standard for all educated people. To fulfill this need, general education curricula were developed to offer students such basic knowledge, as opposed to specialized knowledge acquired later in their chosen technical or professional curricula.

In Europe, higher education began to develop as early as the 11th century. Some of the oldest universities include those established in Bologne, Oxford, and Paris. The goal for European university students was to acquire a basic understanding of the natural world and society at large through Christian disciplines. As the means for pursuing and discussing the truth, students trained in the seven liberal arts: grammar, logic, rhetoric, arithmetic, geometry, astronomy, and music. These subjects can be traced back to ancient Greece, where they were considered essential for a free (or "liberal") person to actively participate in civic life; hence the name "liberal arts." After acquiring the arts, students could go on to study theology in order to pursue an understanding of how the world works.

When Japan modernized its education during the Meiji Restoration, a Germanized version of the European university was introduced to establish what is now the University of Tokyo. At the time, Japan prioritized practical skills and knowledge to the pursuit of truth and enlightenment. Thus, the organization of academic departments was centered more on American-like practical subjects. This mixture of ideas and traditions of both European liberal arts and American general education can still be observed within Japanese higher education institutions today.

(331 Words)

higher education　高等教育
practical learning　実学
Bologne　ボローニャ
the seven liberal arts　自由学芸七科
the Meiji Restoration　明治維新

## ***Exercise 1*** 本文を読んで下の質問に答えましょう。

1. Which is NOT true about higher education in the United States?
   (A) It does not have a long history.
   (B) It had to provide standardized knowledge for educated people.
   (C) Engineering and agriculture were examples of practical subjects taught.
   (D) General education curricula offered students specialized knowledge.

2. What was the goal for European universities?
   (A) To develop old universities in Bologne, Oxford, and Paris
   (B) To have students acquire a fundamental knowledge of the world
   (C) To train students in the seven liberal arts
   (D) To make Christian disciplines great again

3. How is Japanese higher education unique?
   (A) There is a mixture of ideas and traditions within institutions.
   (B) Japan needed more enlightenment than skills.
   (C) European liberal arts were valued.
   (D) Modernized universities were not established.

## ***Exercise 2*** 次の各文が本文の内容に合っていれば **T** を，合っていなければ **F** を選びましょう。

1. **T / F** "The seven liberal arts" means to pursue and discuss the truth.
2. **T / F** The subjects were called "liberal arts" because they were essential for "liberal" citizens.
3. **T / F** The first Japanese universities were established based on the German system.

### 中世ヨーロッパの高等教育と現代の学位

中世ヨーロッパの大学では，自由学芸七科が基礎学力として必須でした。その上位に哲学があり，七科を統合して理論的思考を身に付けるための学問でした。そして，最終段階として神学を研究し，世界の法則性を導こうとしました。実は，この考え方は現代の学位名に受け継がれ，学部卒業で与えられる Bachelor of Arts は「学芸を志す者」，修士修了 Master of Arts は「学芸を修めた者」，博士認定を経た Doctor of Philosophy は「哲学で水準に達した者」というのが元の意味です。

# Writing

## Exercise 1　日本語に合うように（　　）内に適切な語を書き入れましょう。

1. Have (　　　　　　) (　　　　　　) (　　　　　　) stopped speeding?
（スピード違反で止められたことはありますか。）

2. What percentage of the students (　　　　　　) (　　　　　　) (　　　　　　) college?
（生徒の大学進学率はどのくらいですか。）

3. English education is (　　　　　　) (　　　　　　) (　　　　　　) reading and writing.
（英語教育は主に読み書きが中心です。）

## Exercise 2　（　　）内の語を並べかえて英文を完成させましょう。

1. How ( to / did / be / it / that / come ) you both left at the same time?
（どうしてお二人は同時に出掛けることになったのですか。）

______________________________________________

2. The virus was discovered as ( as / year / November / early / last ).

______________________________________________

3. These meats ( for / are / safe / human / considered ) consumption.

______________________________________________

## Exercise 3　本文にある表現を用いて，日本語に合うように英文を完成させましょう。

1. 学校は生徒に制服の着用を求めた。

______________________________________________

2. その伝統は 14 世紀にまで遡る。

______________________________________________

3. 家康は今の愛知県に生まれた。

______________________________________________

# Unit 2

# 3D Ashura

## プロジェクションマッピングの阿修羅

## Listening

### Warm Up

07

**◆ 文アクセント ◆**

文アクセントには，強く発音される content words（内容語）と，弱く発音される function words（機能語）があります（**付録①**を参照)。特に，話者が文中で一番伝えたい情報は最も強く発音します。

Here comes a huge tsunami.

She's working at the British Museum.

| | |
|---|---|
| ★ | 最も強い部分 |
| ● | 強い部分 |
| • | 弱い部分 |

**Exercise 1** 音声を聞いて，何のアイテムの説明かその名前を日本語で（　　）内に書き入れましょう。 08

A（　　　　　　　　　）　B（　　　　　　　　　）　C（　　　　　　　　　）

**Exercise 2** 音声を聞いて，最も適切な応答を一つ選びましょう。 09

1. (A)　(B)　(C)　　2. (A)　(B)　(C)　　3. (A)　(B)　(C)　　4. (A)　(B)　(C)

**Exercise 3** Opening Conversation を聞いて，下の質問に答えましょう。 10

1. Jane と将都は今週末，横浜のどこに行くのか。

______________________________

2. そこで二人は何のショーを見るつもりなのか。

______________________________

# Reading

▶ 英文を読んで質問に答えましょう。

11

Large-scale entertainment facilities called “theme parks” are designed based on the concept that people can enter a fantastic world using their own imagination to escape from their daily lives. Both Tokyo Disneyland and Universal Studios Japan continue to produce new events to entertain people. One of their main targets is to increase the number of their repeat customers.

These theme parks offer various kinds of shows, such as electric parades and spectacular fireworks. In recent years, these parks have started to use a new technology called projection mapping, which has proven to be successful in drawing a great number of people. One example of this for entertainment is the show at Tokyo Disneyland, which features computer-generated images of popular Disney characters projected on the walls of Cinderella’s Castle.

Projection mapping is a new technology that casts images on the walls of buildings with sound effects in darkness. What sets this form of entertainment apart from films is that unlike movies, which can now be viewed on any device at any time, you cannot enjoy the show unless you actually visit the venue. The technology is believed to have been popularized when the “Tokyo Station Vision” was held in 2012. Many people gathered at Tokyo Station to watch the spectacular visual display.

A popular Buddhist image in Nara has been chosen as a subject of projection mapping. The name of the image is Ashura. Its tender face and merciful look have enchanted many people over the centuries. So it is no wonder that Ashura was projected during the Sapporo Snow Festival.

The 3D masterpiece, Ashura, was transported beyond ancient time to modern time, showing the power of perfect expression created by cutting-edge technology. The clear pop-up images were screened on the back of a replica of Kofukuji Temple made of snow blocks. People were able to enjoy the fantastic view for a short time. It might be a good idea to choose the mapping site as a dating spot.

(328 Words)

## Exercise 1 本文を読んで下の質問に答えましょう。

1. What will the theme parks do to have more repeat customers?
   (A) They will continue to break old attractions and make new ones.
   (B) They will construct big machines such as roller coasters.
   (C) They will continue to create new events to entertain many people.
   (D) They will build new buildings periodically to have more customers.

2. What is the unique feature of projection mapping?
   (A) This is a new form of entertainment people can enjoy at music events.
   (B) It is a unique map to find Cinderella Castle at Tokyo Disneyland.
   (C) This is a new machine to cast CG images on screens or flat surfaces.
   (D) It is a new technology to project images on the walls of buildings, etc.

3. Why are the images of Ashura of Kofukuji Temple so popular?
   (A) Because the images appeared at the Sapporo Snow Festival.
   (B) Because the boyish faces of the images look tender and merciful.
   (C) Because the images have the faces of boys, not those of gods.
   (D) Because the images were the most influential ones in the past.

## Exercise 2 次の各文が本文の内容に合っていればTを，合っていなければFを選びましょう。

1. T / F Projection mapping has proven to be a successful technology to attract many people.
2. T / F A visual show called "Tokyo Station Vision" played an important role in making projection mapping popular.
3. T / F A beautiful pop-up image of Kofukuji Temple was screened at the Sapporo Snow Festival.

### プロジェクションマッピング

これはCGIとプロジェクターを用いて，建物などの立体物，あるいは空間に映像を映し出す技術のことです。プロジェクションは「投影する」，マッピングは「映像を張り合わせる」という意味です。欧米などでは，ビデオマッピング，3Dマッピング，ビジュアルマッピングとも呼ばれています。スクリーンのような平面ではなく，立体物に投影することが特徴です。

# Writing

**Exercise 1** 日本語に合うように（　　）内に適切な語を書き入れましょう。

1. Theme parks continue to develop new events to (　　　　　　)(　　　　　　).
(テーマパークは人々を楽しませるために新しいイベントを開発し続けています。)

2. Projection mapping cast images (　　　　　　)(　　　　　　)(　　　　　　).
(プロジェクションマッピングは音響効果とともに映像を投影します。)

3. A 3D masterpiece from the Tempyo era was screened (　　　　　　) time and place.
(天平時代の 3D の傑作が時空を超えて映し出された。)

**Exercise 2** （　　）内の語を並べかえて英文を完成させましょう。

1. People can enjoy the ( world / lives / from / apart / daily / their / fantastic ) at theme parks.
(人々は日常生活と離れた空想の世界をテーマパークで楽しむことができます。)

______________________________________________

2. Projection mapping is ( creates / technology / new / which / a ) three-dimensional images.

______________________________________________

3. You can see ( characters / the walls / Disney / on / popular / the / screened ) of the building.

______________________________________________

**Exercise 3** 本文にある表現を用いて，日本語に合うように英文を完成させましょう。

1. 彼の趣味はテーマパークを訪れることです。

______________________________________________

2. ディズニーのキャラクターがショーに出たことは不思議ではない。

______________________________________________

3. 彼女に誕生日プレゼントをあげるのはいい考えかもしれない。

______________________________________________

# Unit 3

# Korean and Chinese Dramas

アジアドラマの魅力

## Listening

### Warm Up

12

**◆ 音の脱落（1）◆**

話し言葉では，文字にあっても実際には読まれず，聞こえない音として脱落することがあります。音の脱落は，子音連続や破裂音など，隣接する音の環境によって起こります。

| | |
|---|---|
| [t], [d] の脱落 | exactly, next week, kindness, iced coffee |
| [k] の脱落 | picture, asked them, I got stuck with some work. |
| [f] の脱落 | half past nine, a cup of tea ← "かっぱ亭" のように聞こえます。 |

子音＋語頭 [h] の脱落

She likes him.

with heat

Miyabi is her daughter.

＊ [t], [d] のような音は完全に消えるのではなく，「ッ」のように聞こえます。

**Exercise 1** 音声を聞いて，何のアイテムの説明かその名前を日本語で（　　）内に書き入れましょう。 13

A（　　　　　　　　）　B（　　　　　　　　）　C（　　　　　　　　）

**Exercise 2** 音声を聞いて，最も適切な応答を一つ選びましょう。 14

**1.** (A)　(B)　(C)　　**2.** (A)　(B)　(C)　　**3.** (A)　(B)　(C)　　**4.** (A)　(B)　(C)

**Exercise 3** Opening Conversation を聞いて，下の質問に答えましょう。 15

**1.** 雅はどんなジャンルのドラマを見ると言っているか。

____________________________________

**2.** 雅は Gerald にどの撮影場所を勧めているか。

____________________________________

# Reading

▶ 英文を読んで質問に答えましょう。

16

Chinese and Korean dramas, along with Korean music and especially K-pop, have long been popular in Japan. Korea and China have become so popular among Japanese college students that they are now included as study abroad destinations. Current international student programs to Korea incorporate cultural experiences such as eating local cuisine, wearing traditional clothes, and learning K-pop dance moves.

Korean shows feature a variety of themes, ranging from family drama to fantasy. Some weave time travel into their narratives, which allows for specific historical and cultural elements to be depicted. When these shows are reinterpreted in Japan, the historical events and other pertinent details are tailored to suit the cultural context. For example, if the Korean version stars a character who travels back to the Joseon period, the Japanese version will have its hero or heroine travel back to the Edo era.

Chinese dramas tend to be historical, among which a popular motif is "The Three Kingdom Saga." In such dramas, gorgeous costumes and ornaments attract the viewer's attention. Another characteristic is the frequent use of poetry. For example, Li Bai's poems are often cited. Even in modern society, poetry is quoted in daily conversations, and reciting poetry is still prevalent in Chinese culture. Recently, however, dramas based on novels or popular SNS topics are also being produced, and they are gaining popularity among young people.

Another interesting point is that watching Korean and Chinese drama shows often reveals unexpected phonetic characteristics shared by the Japanese, Korean, and Chinese languages. For example, the Japanese sounds of "tea" (cha), "attention" (chūi), "library" (toshokan), "theory" (riron), "grapes" (budō), and "triangular relationships" (sankaku-kankei) are pronounced similarly in Chinese and Korean.

Japanese viewers may be particularly drawn to Korean and Chinese dramas because they have cultural attributes that feel familiar. However, the universal appeal of these drama series is that they allow the viewer to step into another world, accept a fresh perspective, and connect with a different culture that cannot be experienced through the written word alone.

(334 Words)

The Three Kingdom Saga　三国志
Li Bai　李白

**Exercise 1** 本文を読んで下の質問に答えましょう。

1. What is included in the international student programs?
   (A) Tasting Korean dishes
   (B) Trying traditional Korean fashion
   (C) Learning Korean dances
   (D) All of the above

2. According to this passage, what is unique about Korean dramas?
   (A) K-pop songs must be played.
   (B) Their content transcends time and space.
   (C) The main characters are active in the Edo period.
   (D) The heroes became Joseon Dynasty kings.

3. What is unique about Chinese dramas according to this passage?
   (A) They contain many elements of the drama series "The Three Kingdom Saga."
   (B) Gorgeous court costumes are popular among young people.
   (C) Chinese poetry is often quoted in the dramas.
   (D) Li Bai's poems are always quoted in everyday conversations.

**Exercise 2** 次の各文が本文の内容に合っていれば **T** を，合っていなければ **F** を選びましょう。

1. **T / F** Many TV channels broadcast Korean and Chinese dramas.
2. **T / F** There are amazing similarities between Chinese, Japanese, and Korean sounds.
3. **T / F** Japanese viewers may not be interested in Chinese or Korean cultures.

**ドラマの映像技術**

近年の韓国・中国ドラマの作品は，映像技術の発展がめざましく，放送本数やDVDのリリース数が増加している。レンタルショップでも，洋画・邦画の他，アジアドラマ（華流・韓流）が棚を埋め尽くしており，本格的なブームを迎えている。ドラマと聞くと，時代設定や話数の多さなどで避けてしまう人もいるかもしれないが，洋画好きや海外ドラマ好きにも響く要素が含まれている。中国ドラマに関しては，ハリウッド並みの製作費で，一作が100億円規模のものも珍しくない。

# Writing

**Exercise 1** 日本語に合うように（　　）内に適切な語を書き入れましょう。

1. A trip to Busan can be a wonderful (　　　　　　)(　　　　　　).
（釜山旅行は，素晴らしい文化体験となります。）

2. The Japanese (　　　　　　) of the novel has beautiful pictures compared to other (　　　　　　).
（日本版の小説は，他の版に比べて挿絵が素敵です。）

3. (　　　　　　) cultural characteristics were found among the two nations.
（二国間では意外な文化的な特徴が見られました。）

**Exercise 2** （　　）内の語を並べかえて英文を完成させましょう。

1. Concert ticket prices ( ¥3,000 / ¥500 / to / from / range ).
（コンサートチケットの値段は 500 円から 3,000 円です。）

______________________________________________

2. Du Fu's ( are / quoted / poems / often / in ) Chinese dramas.

______________________________________________

3. He came ( of / approach / up / a / with / learning / fresh ) a new language.

______________________________________________

**Exercise 3** 本文にある表現を用いて，日本語に合うように英文を完成させましょう。

1. 歴史ドラマには紫禁城を題材にしたものが多くあります。

______________________________________________

2. アジア諸国には共通の歴史があります。

______________________________________________

3. 韓国ドラマは，伝統的な楽器を使う傾向があります。

______________________________________________

# Unit 4

# Rice Plant

お米の恵み

## Listening

### Warm Up

17

**◆ 音の脱落（2）◆**

自然なスピードの会話では，しばしば音が弱くなり（弱化），音が聞こえなくなることがあります（**付録②**を参照）。特に速い会話では，同じ子音同士や短縮形などで音が脱落します。

You don't eat it.　短縮形 -n't の [t] 脱落

Don't forget to bring your textbook.　同じ子音 [t] の脱落

人称代名詞と be 動詞や助動詞の組み合わせ

you are → you're [jʊə], you will → you'll [juːl]

you would → you'd [juːd], you have → you've [juːv]

**Exercise 1**　音声を聞いて，どの飲食物の説明かその名前を日本語で（　　）内に書き入れましょう。

18

A（　　　　　　　　）　B（　　　　　　　　）　C（　　　　　　　　）

**Exercise 2**　音声を聞いて，最も適切な応答を一つ選びましょう。

19

1. (A)　(B)　(C)　　2. (A)　(B)　(C)　　3. (A)　(B)　(C)　　4. (A)　(B)　(C)

**Exercise 3**　Opening Conversation を聞いて，下の質問に答えましょう。

20

1. 将都が朝食でたいてい食べるものは何か。

______________________________

2. Jane が大好きな日本食は何か。

______________________________

# Reading

▶ 英文を読んで質問に答えましょう。 21

The rice plant is extremely important not only in Japan, but in other countries in Asia as well. It provides us with food and sources of revenue, sustaining food culture.

Rice is the staple food of Japan. We have been growing rice for millennia, and we have even developed biotechnological means to ensure a rich rice harvest, not only because it is vital to feed the country but also because it has been considered as a symbol of fertility since ancient times.

Many Japanese dishes include rice. We cannot prepare the popular curry-and-rice without it, for instance. One, also, can never enjoy the delicacy of sushi without rice. A variety of Chinese dishes are also based on plain rice. Furthermore, Japan has a long tradition of brewing rice wine, called "sake," which is a major industry in Japan.

In medieval Japan, bands of samurai warriors showed their loyalty to their lord in order to win more rice crops. In the modern era, if a natural disaster occurs somewhere, we send rice or rice balls to help the people affected. Recently, the Japanese government sent rice specialists to Africa, where people suffer from food shortages caused by drought. They gave local people aid by growing dry-land rice plants called NERICA.

In addition to African dry climates, Japan has also innovated rice strains that can grow in cold climates. For example, it was impossible to grow rice in Hokkaido because of cold weather. A group of researchers, however, developed a cold-resistant species, *Yumepirika*, after a long-term crossing process. Now, *Yumepirika* from Hokkaido has established its popularity as one of the major brands on the market.

Lately, Japanese people have been eating more bread than rice, but the latter is still the principal ingredient of the national diet. At the same time, rice is now recognized internationally as being very healthy, and the large number of sushi restaurants throughout the world tells us that rice may also play an important role in food culture abroad.

(332 Words)

biotechnological means　バイオ技術
bands of samurai warriors　武士団
dry-land rice plant　陸稲
NERICA　New Rice for Africa

## Exercise 1 本文を読んで下の質問に答えましょう。

1. Which of the following statements is true?
   (A) Rice is not important in Japan but only in other Asian countries.
   (B) People have developed biotechnology to reduce the annual rice harvest.
   (C) Rice is the principal food of the national diet in Japan.
   (D) People regard a good rice harvest as a symbol of rich farmers.

2. Why is rice beneficial for us? * beneficial: 有益な
   (A) Because it is a basic food for Japanese and Chinese dishes.
   (B) Because it can be a great help for starving people to survive.
   (C) Because we can make a large amount of alcoholic drinks from it.
   (D) All of the above

3. Which of the following statements is NOT true?
   (A) It was too cold to grow rice Hokkaido in the past.
   (B) *Yumepirika* is a new brand which is grown in Hokkaido.
   (C) Japanese have been eating much more rice than bread in recent years.
   (D) Rice is a very important food at sushi restaurants around the world.

## Exercise 2 次の各文が本文の内容に合っていれば T を，合っていなければ F を選びましょう。

1. **T / F** Rice is an essential crop in many ways for the people in Asia, including Japan.
2. **T / F** The rice wine brewing industry is no longer a major business in modern Japan.
3. **T / F** People understand that rice is a very healthy food, and sushi restaurants around the world attract customers.

### ご飯の魅力

米の消費は，1950 年代の 3 分の 1 以下になったと言われています。ご飯はパン，パスタ，ラーメンなど他の食品におされ，食べる機会が減っています。しかし，私たちは食の多様性を享受する一方で，ふっくら炊いたご飯の食感に魅せられている人は多いようです。すし飯と和食用のご飯では使う米や，米を水に浸す時間が違うなど，炊き方ひとつにも洗練された日本の食文化の技が込められています。

# Writing

**Exercise 1** 日本語に合うように（　　）内に適切な語を書き入れましょう。

1. We have (　　　　　　) (　　　　　　) rice for more than a thousand year.
   （私たちは千年以上，お米を栽培してきました。）

2. We (　　　　　　) brew rice wine (　　　　　　) rice.
   （お米がなければ日本酒を作ることができません。）

3. Hokkaido is now a major place (　　　　　　) farmers produce the brand rice.
   （北海道は今や農家がブランド米を生産する主要な産地です。）

**Exercise 2** （　　）内の語を並べかえて英文を完成させましょう。

1. The rice is important not only because it is the staple food ( sustains / also / it / because / culture / but / food ).
   （お米は主食としてだけではなく，食文化を支えているので重要です。）

   ______________________________________________

2. We send rice to the ( are / from / people / suffering / who ) food shortages.

   ______________________________________________

3. It was ( grow / to / weather / impossible / rice / cold / in ) in the past.

   ______________________________________________

**Exercise 3** 本文にある表現を用いて，日本語に合うように英文を完成させましょう。

1. お米は様々な日本料理を作るのに必要な食材です。

   ______________________________________________

2. 日本料理は健康的であると認識されています。

   ______________________________________________

3. 世界中の寿司店はおいしい寿司を出します。

   ______________________________________________

# Unit 5

# A Thousand Years of Love

千年の恋物語

## Listening

### Warm Up

22

**◆ 音の同化 ◆**

音と音が合わさると，聞こえるはずの音が聞こえなくなることがあります。英語話者は意識せずに発音していますが，日本人の耳では聞き取りにくい音です。音の現象を理解して発音することが大事です。

[j] があとに続く場合　例）[t] + you, [d] + you

How about you?　Did you know her?
[ʧ]　[ʤ]

複数形や 3 人称単数の “~s”

[s] books, T-shirts, cups　無声音の場合は [s] と発音する
[z] goods, brands, wines　有声音の場合は [z] と発音する

**Exercise 1** 音声を聞いて，何の説明かその名前を日本語で（　）内に書き入れましょう。 23

A（　　　　　　）B（　　　　　　）C（　　　　　　）

**Exercise 2** 音声を聞いて，最も適切な応答を一つ選びましょう。 24

1. (A) (B) (C)　2. (A) (B) (C)　3. (A) (B) (C)　4. (A) (B) (C)

**Exercise 3** Opening Conversation を聞いて，下の質問に答えましょう。 25

1. 七夕はどの国のロマンチックな伝説と深い関わりがあるのか。

______________________________

2. 織姫と牽牛《けんぎゅう》はどこを渡って一年に一度会えるのか。

______________________________

# Reading

▶ 英文を読んで質問に答えましょう。

26

People have been interested in romantic stories since ancient times. In ancient Egypt, the love affairs of Cleopatra must have attracted public attention together with her dramatic death. William Shakespeare's *Romeo and Juliet* is probably the most popular love story in the world. Though Romeo and Juliet loved each other, unfortunately, their love didn't go as they desired. The story ends with the lovers' double suicide.

In Japan there remains the sad story of Joruri-hime and Yoshitsune. According to the legend, about one thousand years ago, Yoshitsune fell in love with Joruri-hime when he listened to the beautiful melody of her koto playing. Yoshitsune immediately started to play his flute in reply to the koto tune. The two lovers struggled with overwhelming hardships. You will find the name of Joruri in the traditional puppet show called ningyo-joruri.

Meanwhile, Yoshitsune was an heir of the Genji clan and a well-known character who defeated the Heike clan. However, people regard him as a tragic hero in history because he was killed by pursuers sent by his elder brother. The tragedy of Yoshitsune has traditionally been re-enacted in the form of plays such as kabuki. His man, Benkei, managed to save his lord in a smart manner in the "Kanjin-cho," which was a popular kabuki program. It is said that the story expresses the most fascinating aspects of human nature.

Since parting is such sweet sorrow, Joruri-hime tried to follow Yoshitsune, but in vain. It might be her destiny that a young girl could not stay together with Yoshitsune for the rest of her life. Actually, she was forced to return home by her father. Finally, she is said to have thrown herself into the Oto River because she couldn't wait for her lover for such a long time. Her suicidal point in the river is known as "Joruri's Abyss," which is now a scenic spot for tourists, together with her tomb and memorial monuments.

(322 Words)

Joruri-hime　浄瑠璃姫
Yoshitsune　源義経
puppet show　文楽
ningyo-joruri　人形浄瑠璃
Benkei　弁慶
Kanjin-cho　勧進帳
Oto River　乙川
Joruri's Abyss　浄瑠璃が淵

## *Exercise* 1 本文を読んで下の質問に答えましょう。

1. What happened with *Romeo and Juliet* at the end of the story?
   (A) Romeo and Juliet loved each other and got married at last.
   (B) Only Romeo committed suicide in the last part of the story.
   (C) Juliet died at the end of the story though Romeo tried to save her.
   (D) Both Romeo and Juliet killed themselves at the end of the story.

2. Which of the following statements is true according to the legend?
   (A) Yoshitsune started to play his flute in order to distract Joruri-hime.
   (B) Yoshitsune fell in love with Joruri-hime from her beautiful koto melody.
   (C) Joruri-hime fell in love with Yoshitsune when she listened to his flute.
   (D) Joruri-hime was performing a puppet show when Yoshitsune visited her.

3. How did the romance between Joruri-hime and Yoshitsune come to an end?
   (A) Joruri-hime tried to kill herself but Yoshitsune saved her life.
   (B) Both Joruri-hime and Yoshitsune killed themselves in a river.
   (C) Joruri-hime killed herself and Yoshitsune was killed by his pursuers.
   (D) Yoshitsune and his men were killed but Joruri-hime survived.

## *Exercise* 2 次の各文が本文の内容に合っていれば **T** を，合っていなければ **F** を選びましょう。

1. **T / F** Joruri-hime sometimes played her part in the puppet show, ningyo-joruri.
2. **T / F** The story of Yoshitune was included in kabuki programs after his death.
3. **T / F** Some tourists visit “Joruri’s Abyss” and other related sites of Joruri-hime.

### 浄瑠璃姫伝説

浄瑠璃姫は，三河国矢作の里の長者の娘で，源氏の御曹司である源義経（牛若丸）と出会い，相思相愛の仲になる。しかし，源氏再興をめざす義経は姫のもとを去ってしまう。果たせぬ恋と悟り，姫は川に身を投げてしまう。一方，義経は壇ノ浦で平氏を滅亡させたものの，兄頼朝の謀略により，奥州平泉で最期を遂げる。この悲しい恋物語がSNSやインターネットなどで広まり，若い女性などが姫ゆかりの地を訪れています。

## Writing

**Exercise 1** 日本語に合うように（　　）内に適切な語を書き入れましょう。

1. She must (　　　　　　) (　　　　　　) the ending of the love story.
   (彼女はそのラブストーリーの結末を知っていたに違いない。)

2. (　　　　　　) (　　　　　　) legend, Yoshitsune visited here on his journey.
   (伝説によれば，義経が旅の途中ここを訪れた。)

3. He tried to solve the problem by himself, but (　　　　　　) (　　　　　　).
   (彼はひとりで問題を解決しようとしたが無駄だった。)

**Exercise 2** （　　）内の語を並べかえて英文を完成させましょう。

1. He ( first / in / with / love / at / fell / her ) sight.
   (彼は彼女に一目ぼれした。)

   ______________________________

2. The stories of romance have ( told / ancient / from / times / been ).

   ______________________________

3. It ( she / that / is / well-known / is / said / a ) tragic heroine in history.

   ______________________________

**Exercise 3** 本文にある表現を用いて，日本語に合うように英文を完成させましょう。

1. 二人の若い恋人たちの悲しい物語が残っています。

   ______________________________

2. 彼女は最もよく知られたヒロインの一人だとみなされています。

   ______________________________

3. 浄瑠璃姫の物語は演劇という形態で再現されてきました。

   ______________________________

# Unit 6

# Coming to America

## アメリカからの手紙

## Listening

### Warm Up

27

◆ 音の連結（リンキング）◆

英語は自然なスピードで話す時，語尾の子音と語頭の母音が連結することがあります。これをリンキングと呼びます。

| | | |
|---|---|---|
| 1. | Have you done it?（ダニット） | [n]＋母音 |
| 2. | The weather will clear up soon.（クレアラップ） | [r]＋母音 |
| 3. | There are four of us.（ゼアラ） | [r]＋母音 |
| 4. | Let's sing a song now.（シンガァソン） | [ŋ]＋母音 |
| 5. | Did you come up with a new idea?（カマップウィズ） | [m]＋母音 |

**Exercise 1** 音声を聞いて，何の説明かその名前を日本語で（　　）内に書き入れましょう。 28

A（　　　　　　　　　）　B（　　　　　　　　　）　C（　　　　　　　　　）

**Exercise 2** 音声を聞いて，最も適切な応答を一つ選びましょう。 29

1. (A)　(B)　(C)　　2. (A)　(B)　(C)　　3. (A)　(B)　(C)　　4. (A)　(B)　(C)

**Exercise 3** Opening Conversation を聞いて，下の質問に答えましょう。 30

1. 佑子はどうして悲しんでいるのか。

______________________________

2. David はどんなアドバイスをしているのか。

______________________________

# Reading

▶ 英文を読んで質問に答えましょう。 31

Dear Yuko,

How are you? I imagine that the cherry blossoms are already blooming over there as you read this. Connecticut is a lot colder than Japan so spring has yet to arrive here.

It has been a few months since I moved and I am slowly getting used to this new way of life. I live in a quiet part of town that is known for having big, Victorian houses which have been converted into apartments. The houses are beautiful but they are also over 100 years old. In fact, I have already met my landlord several times because he has had to make so many small repairs! But the apartment is quite cozy and there is loads of space.

Speaking of space, it is quite inconvenient to live here without a car because everything is so far apart. Not only are groceries and shops about a 30-minute drive from where I live, but it gets unbelievably cold here in the winter! I experienced my first ever Nor'easter last December—that is apparently what storms along the East Coast of North America are called.

Now that I have a much bigger kitchen, I am cooking every day. It is actually fun to shop at Trader Joe's and local farmer's markets to get fresh produce and it's healthier to cook your own food. There are many cafes and restaurants around but it can get pretty pricey, especially since you have to tip your servers here.

Despite not having to deal with language barriers, I am, unsurprisingly, experiencing culture shock. But the wonderful thing about the United States is that you really do get to meet people from all over the world who are also going through the same challenges. And I am so grateful for friends like you who make me feel loved and supported even though we are far apart.

Let me know when you are free to chat over Zoom.

Love,
MK

(324 Words)

## Exercise 1　本文を読んで下の質問に答えましょう。

1. Who wrote the message?
    (A) Yuko's student
    (B) Yuko's sister
    (C) Yuko's friend
    (D) Somebody Yuko does not know well

2. Where does the sender live now?
    (A) Connecticut
    (B) Victoria
    (C) Trader Joe's
    (D) Nor'easter

3. What does the sender say about her new life?
    (A) She doesn't like her apartment because it is very small and old.
    (B) She likes going to many local restaurants that serve fresh food.
    (C) She has never had any problem adjusting to a new culture.
    (D) She is taking her time to get accustomed to her new life.

## Exercise 2　次の各文が本文の内容に合っていれば T を，合っていなければ F を選びましょう。

1. T / F　The apartment the sender lives in is very old and needed a lot of fixing.
2. T / F　The area where the sender lives never had a storm until last December.
3. T / F　The sender is good at communicating in the language spoken in the new place.

### チップ

チップは，日本ではあまりなじみがありませんが，アメリカやヨーロッパでは欠かすことのできないものです。アメリカのレストランやカフェでは，地域にもよりますが，代金の 15% から 20% のチップをつけるのが慣例です。クレジット払いのときにも，チップの金額を入力します。セルフサービスのフードコートやファストフード店ではチップは特には必要ありません。

# Writing

## Exercise 1 日本語に合うように（　　）内に適切な語を書き入れましょう。

1. I hope you are having fun (　　　　　　) (　　　　　　).
   （そちらで楽しんでいることと思います。）

2. They watched (　　　　　　) (　　　　　　) movies over the weekend.
   （彼らは週末にたくさん映画を見た。）

3. (　　　　　　) (　　　　　　) the vacation is over, you should study hard.
   （休みは終わったのだから，しっかりと勉強すべきだ。）

## Exercise 2 （　　）内の語を並べかえて英文を完成させましょう。

1. That is a question that ( to / yet / be / has / answered ).
   （それは，まだ答えが得られていない質問だ。）

   ______________________________

2. He ( TV / watch / gets / until / to ) 11 o'clock.

   ______________________________

3. I ( assistance / so / for / am / grateful / your ).

   ______________________________

## Exercise 3 本文にある表現を用いて，日本語に合うように英文を完成させましょう。

1. 城はホテルへと転換された。

   ______________________________

2. 劇場は学校から徒歩 15 分のところにある。

   ______________________________

3. 私たちは電話で議論した。

   ______________________________

# Unit 7

# Aqua Blue

スキューバダイビングに挑戦

## Listening

### Warm Up

32

◆ 音の弱形（機能語と内容語）◆

音の強弱では強い音だけでなく，弱い音（曖昧な音 [ə]）を意識することも重要です。音が弱化することで，同化や脱落が生じます。例えば，店員さんにメニューで “Soup or salad?” と聞かれた際，“or” の部分が弱化するため，スーパーサラダのようにひとつの語のように聞こえます。

soup or salad　　milk and sugar　　go away

ring of fire　　heard of it

**Exercise 1**　音声を聞いて，どのスポーツの説明か，スポーツ名を日本語で（　　）内に書き入れましょう。　33

A（　　　　　　　　）　B（　　　　　　　　）　C（　　　　　　　　）

**Exercise 2**　音声を聞いて，最も適切な応答を一つ選びましょう。　34

1. (A)　(B)　(C)　　2. (A)　(B)　(C)　　3. (A)　(B)　(C)　　4. (A)　(B)　(C)

**Exercise 3**　Opening Conversation を聞いて，下の質問に答えましょう。　35

1. David はダイビングスポットとして，太平洋側のどこを勧めているのか。

______________________________

2. ダイビング合宿の実地訓練では何の使い方を習うのか。

______________________________

▶ 英文を読んで質問に答えましょう。

36

If you are seeking an adventure in the blue ocean, taking up scuba diving might be the perfect activity for you. Scuba diving is one of the world's fast growing and most exciting marine sports. Diving underwater, swimming while breathing with the aid of an air tank, momentarily experiencing atmospheric pressure—these are things you can never experience aboveground.

Masato and David traveled to Okinawa in order to improve their ability to control neutral buoyancy this summer. Last year, they joined a training camp to obtain a scuba diving license at Miyake-jima Island, learning the basic skills and acquiring general knowledge about the sport and the ocean. The more they learned, the more curious they became about the wonders and dangers of the ocean.

On their first day in Okinawa, Jennifer, their instructor, took the two boys to a shallow diving spot to see tropical fish. David was quite surprised to see a clownfish hiding among the sea anemone. "That fish must be Nemo from the Disney film." He sent hand signs with excitement. Masato and David felt as if they were in an ocean paradise, surrounded by an endless variety of tropical fish.

On their second day, Jennifer guided Masato and David to a particular spot of the water, some 10 to 20 meters in depth, to practice neutral buoyancy. Masato began to feel the increasing water pressure on his whole body as he swam towards the ocean floor. Jennifer trained them how to keep their neutral buoyancy, swimming at different depths.

On the last day of their trip, Jennifer showed the two boys photos to educate them about the crises related to the ocean. Actually, she was a greenie and a member of an environmental group in Australia called Planet Ark. They came to realize how much the ocean needed their help. Masato and David not only practiced their diving techniques, they also learned about important issues such as ocean plastics and marine debris.

(326 Words)

Miyake-jima Island　三宅島（伊豆七島のひとつ）
Planet Ark　オーストラリアの環境保護団体

## Exercise 1 本文を読んで下の質問に答えましょう。

1. What would you experience if you took up scuba diving?
   (A) You would feel as if you suddenly jumped from an airplane.
   (B) You would feel more atmospheric pressure than on the ground.
   (C) You would enjoy underwater swimming without an air supply from a tank.
   (D) Scuba diving would give you exactly the same experience as on the ground.

2. Why did Masato and David visit Okinawa this summer?
   (A) To get a scuba diving license
   (B) To view colorful tropical fish
   (C) To improve their buoyancy technique
   (D) To acquire basic knowledge about the sport

3. What did Masato and David experience through the diving trip to Okinawa?
   (A) They got excited when they saw various tropical fish in the sea.
   (B) They practiced their neutral buoyancy technique.
   (C) They learned about marine pollution from Jennifer.
   (D) All of the above

## Exercise 2 次の各文が本文の内容に合っていれば **T** を，合っていなければ **F** を選びましょう。

1. **T / F** Scuba diving is becoming popular world-wide as one of the most exciting marine sports.
2. **T / F** While they were at the training camp, Masato and David were interested in diving techniques, but not the wonders and dangers of the ocean.
3. **T / F** Jennifer taught Masato and David about marine pollution problems as well as diving techniques.

### スキューバダイビング

スキューバダイビングは，中性浮力（浮きも沈みもしない状態）を常に保つことが基本です。浮力の変化に応じて，ダイビングギアでジャケット内の空気を出し入れして調整します。海中では安全を確保するために，時々，深度計・残圧計・コンパスを確認しながら行動します。深くなればなるほど，タンク内の空気の消費量が増えるので，特に注意が必要です。

# Writing

**Exercise 1** 日本語に合うように（　　）内に適切な語を書き入れましょう。

1. He decided to (　　　　　　) (　　　　　　) swimming for his health.
（彼は健康のため，水泳を始めることを決めた。）

2. That fish (　　　　　　) (　　　　　　) a popular tropical fish.
（その魚は人気の熱帯魚に違いない。）

3. They felt (　　　　　　) (　　　　　　) they were in a fantastic world.
（彼らはまるで空想の世界にいるかのように感じた。）

**Exercise 2** （　　）内の語を並べかえて英文を完成させましょう。

1. Do you know ( aid / to / of / breathe / the / how / with ) an air tank?
（空気タンクを使って呼吸する仕方を知っていますか。）

______________________________________________

2. The instructor took ( spot / to / them / the / diving ) by boat.

______________________________________________

3. They began ( increasing / the / dive, / water / feeling / to / pressure ).

______________________________________________

**Exercise 3** 本文にある表現を用いて，日本語に合うように英文を完成させましょう。

1. ダイビングは地上ではできないことが体験できる。

______________________________________________

2. 深く潜れば潜るほど，強い水圧を感じます。

______________________________________________

3. 彼女は海に関わる危機を彼らに教えた。

______________________________________________

# Unit 8

# Roman Numerals

ローマ数字

## Listing

## Listening

### Warm Up

37

◆ 数字の読み方 ◆

英語の数字の読み方を確認しましょう。

大きな数字の読み方：127,817,277　少数点がある場合：42.195

西暦の読み方：the 1700s（1700 年代），the 1920s（1920 年代），2000，2009

分数：2/3 two thirds，1/5 one fifth，1/10 one tenth，1/4 a quarter

**Exercise 1**　音声を聞いて，どんな科目か，その名前を日本語で（　　）内に書き入れましょう。 38

A（　　　　　　　）　B（　　　　　　　）　C（　　　　　　　）

**Exercise 2**　音声を聞いて，最も適切な応答を一つ選びましょう。 39

1. (A)　(B)　(C)　　2. (A)　(B)　(C)　　3. (A)　(B)　(C)　　4. (A)　(B)　(C)

**Exercise 3**　Opening Conversation を聞いて，下の質問に答えましょう。 40

1. 雅は何を見ていたのか。

______________________________

2. 今度の国王の名前は何になったのか。

______________________________

# Reading

▶ 英文を読んで質問に答えましょう。

41

According to *The Oxford English Dictionary*, a numeral is "a figure or character denoting a number." Wherever there is anything to be counted, you would need numbers, along with numerals, to do so. There have been many forms, throughout history, including Chinese, Arabic, and Roman numerals.

Japanese readers should be accustomed to Chinese numerals, as they are what we use within the Japanese system when using Chinese characters. Arabic numerals are also familiar as the numeral script utilized in daily life. However, Roman numerals are not as recognizable. Although Roman numerals were devised some 2,500 years ago, they have not disappeared and are still in use today.

Roman numerals use symbols from the Latin, or Roman, alphabet to represent numbers. Seven basic symbols are employed: I symbolizing *one*, V symbolizing *five*, X symbolizing *ten*, L symbolizing *fifty*, C symbolizing *a hundred*, D symbolizing *five hundred*, and M symbolizing *a thousand*. These basic symbols are combined to denote all other numbers. The general rule is to write the symbols from left to right, or according to the writing system being used. They are arranged by numerical value, going from large to small, adding together the corresponding values. For example, 1537 would be written as MDXXXVII (1000+500+10+10+10+5+1+1). Another rule applies to expressing numbers that involve '4' or '9.' Subtraction is signified by writing a single symbol for the number to be subtracted before the symbol for a larger one. This rule gives you MCMXCIV for 1994 (1000+(1000-100)+(100-10)+(5-1)).

Presently, Arabic numerals have taken the place of Roman numerals, as they are much more practical in everyday use. However, we still see Roman numerals on the face of clocks or in itemized lists. They are used to paginate book attachments. The Statue of Liberty holds in its left hand a tablet with "JULY IV MDCCLXXVI" on it, which is the date of the US Declaration of Independence. It is also interesting to note that Roman numerals were used in earlier books to indicate the year of publication.

(333 Words)

**Exercise 1** 本文を読んで下の質問に答えましょう。

1. Why are Arabic numerals familiar?
   (A) They are used together with Chinese characters.
   (B) They are a part of Roman script.
   (C) They are used widely in daily life.
   (D) They were invented 2,500 years ago.

2. Why have Arabic numerals taken the place of Roman numerals?
   (A) They are easier and much more convenient.
   (B) They can be seen on people's faces.
   (C) They were used to count presents.
   (D) They were attached to book pages.

3. What does "JULY IV MDCCLXXVI" signify?
   (A) It is something left on a statue's hand.
   (B) It is the serial number of a tablet device.
   (C) It is a random selection of Roman numerals.
   (D) It is the Independence Day of the United States.

**Exercise 2** 次の各文が本文の内容に合っていれば **T** を，合っていなければ **F** を選びましょう。

1. **T / F** The only numerals used in the past were Chinese, Arabic, and Roman numerals.
2. **T / F** Only some of the Roman numerals were invented by the Romans.
3. **T / F** In the Roman numeral system, most numbers are represented by a combination of seven basic symbols.

**ローマ数字の使用**

英文中によく見られる表記に WWII があります。これは World War II のことで，II は "two" と読みます。他によく使うローマ数字には，王名の代数表示があります。例えば，フランス王の Louis XVI は，音読のときには "Louis the sixteenth" と読みます。王族に限らず，John Rockefeller IV は石油王ロックフェラー一族 4 人目の John です。クラシック音楽の世界でも，Johann Strauss III は著名な指揮者です。

# Writing

**Exercise 1** 日本語に合うように（　　）内に適切な語を書き入れましょう。

1. He has become (　　　　　　) (　　　　　　) living in a foreign country.
（彼は外国暮らしに慣れてきた。）

2. Please tell us (　　　　　　) (　　　　　　).
（出発するときに声をかけてください。）

3. Tablet devices have (　　　　　　) (　　　　　　) (　　　　　　) (　　　　　　) laptops in this university.
（この大学ではタブレット端末がノートパソコンに取って代わった。）

**Exercise 2** （　　）内の語を並べかえて英文を完成させましょう。

1. This castle fell during ( ago / disturbance / years / the / 150 / some ).
（この城は，150 年ほど前の動乱で崩れた。）

______________________________________________

2. Old Japanese manuscripts are written ( the top / to / of / from / the bottom ) the page.

______________________________________________

3. It ( is / see / sad / also / to / quite / some ) of the systems going out of use.

______________________________________________

**Exercise 3** 本文にある表現を用いて，日本語に合うように英文を完成させましょう。

1. 学生がいるところには，どこにでも食堂が必要となる。

______________________________________________

2. 今建設中の建物が市役所だ。

______________________________________________

3. 柔道の段は帯の色で示される。

______________________________________________

# Unit 9

# Visiting Boston

アフリカ系アメリカ人の歴史探訪

## Listening

### Warm Up

42

**◆英語らしい響き（緊張母音と弛緩母音）◆**

英語の母音は，日本語よりも種類が多く，口の形が大きく変化します。口元を緊張させて発音する緊張母音と緩めて発音する弛緩母音があります。例えば，日本語に似た「イ」は横に口を伸ばして出す音や，「ウ」は唇をすぼめて出す音があります。**付録**にある口の形の図を参考に練習しましょう。（**付録③**参照）

| | | |
|---|---|---|
| 緊張母音 | /i/ | **ea**sy, sp**ee**ch, fr**ee** |
| | /u/ | r**u**le, d**u**ty, val**ue** |
| 弛緩母音 | /ɪ/ | **i**mage, kn**i**t, happ**y** |
| | /ʊ/ | b**oo**k, p**u**sh, h**oo**d |

**Exercise 1** 音声を聞いて，何の説明か，その名前を日本語で（　　）内に書き入れましょう。 43

A（　　　　　　　　）　B（　　　　　　　　）　C（　　　　　　　　）

**Exercise 2** 音声を聞いて，最も適切な応答を一つ選びましょう。 44

1. (A)　(B)　(C)　　2. (A)　(B)　(C)　　3. (A)　(B)　(C)　　4. (A)　(B)　(C)

**Exercise 3** Opening Conversation を聞いて，下の質問に答えましょう。 45

1. Richard は，春休みに何をする予定なのか。

______________________________

2. Richard は，目的地まではどれくらい時間がかかると話しているか。

______________________________

# Reading

▶ 英文を読んで質問に答えましょう。

46

Boston is an essential place to visit if you want to explore the history of the United States. Founded by Puritans in 1630, it is one of the oldest cities in the country. The city has many historical sites related to the American Revolution, including the Boston Tea Party in 1773. The city has excellent museums, prestigious universities, and the old residence of famous writers like Ralph Waldo Emerson and Louisa May Alcott on the outskirts of the city. Boston is also the home of many firsts in the United States: the first public park in 1634, the first public school in 1635, the first subway system in 1897, and the first large public library in 1848.

There are many ways for you to get around the city. You can enjoy walking on your own with a map, sign in for a guided tour, try a hop-on hop-off trolley or a duck boat, take a harbor sightseeing cruise, and so forth. Because of the recent restrictions on tourism, you may also take a virtual tour of the city on the Internet.

The tour along the Black Heritage Trail might also be an interesting option for you. The north side of the Beacon Hill area had been the residential center of the African-American community before President Abraham Lincoln issued the Emancipation Proclamation in 1863. The community grew as some of the many African Americans who were enslaved in southern plantations freed themselves from slavery and moved north to live together as a community.

The community sought more opportunities to gain equal rights as American citizens, and they provided shelters to fugitive slaves. The tour leads you to the most important house for the freedom seekers, built along a narrow walkway which they used in the evening, avoiding the eyes of the public. The tour also takes you to another important first in Boston: the Abiel Smith School, the first public school for freed African-American children, established in 1835.

(327 Words)

逃亡奴隷が利用した狭い通路につながる扉

the Emancipation Proclamation　奴隷解放宣言

## Exercise 1 本文を読んで下の質問に答えましょう。

1. According to the passage, what is a good reason to go to Boston?
   (A) It is a small, traditional city with the best tea shops.
   (B) It is a large city with many international companies.
   (C) It is a metropolitan city with tall skyscrapers.
   (D) It is a historic city with many sightseeing spots.

2. According to the passage, what can visitors do in Boston?
   (A) They can take a self-guided tour around the city.
   (B) They can enjoy going to theme parks.
   (C) They can get on a boat and feed waterbirds.
   (D) They can only take a city tour online.

3. Why has Boston been important for African Americans?
   (A) Famous African-American writers used to live in the city.
   (B) Those who fled from the south built a community in the city.
   (C) Abraham Lincoln used to visit the city to encourage slaves.
   (D) There have been many schools for international residents.

## Exercise 2 次の各文が本文の内容に合っていれば T を，合っていなければ F を選びましょう。

1. T / F The first public park in the United States was created in Boston in the 17th century.
2. T / F Every person of African descent was enslaved in the U.S. before 1863.
3. T / F Runaway slaves could enjoy their freedom in the North without any worry.

### フリーダム・トレイル

ボストンには，フリーダム・トレイル（the Freedom Trail）と呼ばれる道があります。通りに一筋の赤いレンガがまっすぐに敷かれており，そこをたどっていくと，アメリカの独立戦争にゆかりのある 16 か所の名所を訪れることができます。ツアーに参加すれば，18 世紀当時の衣装を身にまとったガイドが案内してくれます。イギリスからの独立を求めて戦った人々の軌跡は，自由の国アメリカの起源を示しています。

# Writing

## Exercise 1　日本語に合うように（　　）内に適切な語を書き入れましょう。

1. Both Miyabi and Yuno live (　　　　　) the outskirts of the city.
   (雅も悠乃も街の郊外に住んでいます。)
2. You might get around the U.S. (　　　　　) (　　　　　) (　　　　　) because you speak English very well.
   (英語がとても上手に話せるので，ひとりでアメリカを回っても良いかもしれません。)
3. We'd like to (　　　　　) in for a walking tour this afternoon.
   (午後のウォーキング・ツアーに参加したいです。)

## Exercise 2　（　　）内の語を並べかえて英文を完成させましょう。

1. Salem ( place / might / to / be / an / visit / interesting ) if you want to learn about witch trials.
   (魔女裁判のことが知りたいなら，セーラムに行くのも良いかもしれないね。)

   ______________________________________________

2. In business, it is ( yourself / important / from / free / to ) the traditional mindset.

   ______________________________________________

3. This ( shops / to / will / you / some / street / lead ) that sell gifts and souvenirs.

   ______________________________________________

## Exercise 3　本文にある表現を用いて，日本語に合うように英文を完成させましょう。

1. ボストンからニューヨークに行くには，3つの方法があります。

   ______________________________________________

2. アメリカ史の授業を取るのは，良い選択ですね。

   ______________________________________________

3. 戦争を生き抜いたわずかな人たちは，無事に故郷に帰りました。

   ______________________________________________

# Unit 10

# Jazz

ジャズの魅力

## Listening

### Warm Up

47

**◆ 子音：息の使い方（帯気音）◆**

英語の破裂音 /p/, /t/, /k/, /b/, /d/, /g/ の中で，特に無声音 [p], [t], [k] は日本語に比べて息の量が異なります。例えば，パ行の音「ピン」よりも，英語の “pin” は勢いよく弾くような音が産出されます。アクセントのある音節の頭に来る無声破裂音が帯気音になります。この帯気音は息の量を意識して，カタカナ発音にならないように練習しましょう。

pin, apartment, tea, eighteen, kick, cook

**Exercise 1** 音声を聞いて，どの楽器の説明か，その楽器名を日本語で（　　）内に書き入れましょう。

48

A（　　　　　　　　）　B（　　　　　　　　）　C（　　　　　　　　）

**Exercise 2** 音声を聞いて，最も適切な応答を一つ選びましょう。

49

**1.** (A)　(B)　(C)　　**2.** (A)　(B)　(C)　　**3.** (A)　(B)　(C)　　**4.** (A)　(B)　(C)

**Exercise 3** Opening Conversation を聞いて，下の質問に答えましょう。

50

**1.** Bob の好きなジャズミュージシャンは誰と誰か。

______________________________________________

**2.** Bob は悠乃にどのジャズの曲を聞くように勧めたのか。

______________________________________________

# Reading

▶ 英文を読んで質問に答えましょう。

51

Jazz is a unique genre of music that has become quite popular throughout the world. It originated in the United States. You may have heard the relaxing tones of jazz being played on a street corner or inside a coffee shop. Adults have more chances to listen to jazz than those from younger generations because it is often played at bars and nightclubs where alcoholic drinks are served.

The most distinctive feature of jazz is its rhythm. The term "swing" characterizes jazz, a rhythm in which the beats that are usually weak are emphasized. Just listen to the standard track number "Take Five," and you will be enchanted with its rhythmic sounds. The saxophone player deliberately shifts the normal metrical accent to change its rhythm.

The saxophone is an essential part of the jazz ensemble, along with the trumpet, the bass guitar, and the piano. People say that the saxophone sounds similar to the human voice because of its mild tone. The saxophone was actually invented around the same time that jazz was born. The sounds of the saxophone truly complement the elements of jazz—this is probably why jazz bands always include the saxophone.

Jazz has the power to stimulate the human brain in ways that awaken its pleasure centers. Its distinctive melody, rhythm, and tempo is able to invoke different moods and feelings. Some jazz pieces can even help alleviate depression or nervousness because of their relaxing effects. This is why jazz is often used as ambient music in offices, waiting rooms, and even elevators.

There is nothing like going to a live jazz performance. Being able to listen to talented musicians improvise and riff off each other can be the experience of a lifetime because each performance is unique and cannot be replicated. If you are a music-lover, the wonderful world of jazz is certainly worth exploring.

(310 Words)

## *Exercise* 1　本文を読んで下の質問に答えましょう。

1. Which of these is true about jazz?
   - (A) Jazz is a relaxing music created for adults only.
   - (B) Jazz is a unique type of music created in America.
   - (C) There is not a specific rhythm called “swing” in jazz.
   - (D) The saxophone player always keeps normal metric accent.

2. Which of these instruments is not included in a jazz ensemble?
   - (A) The violin
   - (B) The trumpet
   - (C) The saxophone
   - (D) The piano

3. Which of these is true about live jazz performances?
   - (A) It is no use going to a live jazz performance.
   - (B) Talented musicians will never improvise and riff off each other.
   - (C) A live jazz performance will never be the experience of a lifetime.
   - (D) You will never hear the same performance twice.

## *Exercise* 2　次の各文が本文の内容に合っていれば **T** を，合っていなければ **F** を選びましょう。

1. **T / F**　Young people have no chance to enjoy jazz because it is always played at places where alcoholic drinks are served.
2. **T / F**　Jazz pieces are no help when you are depressed or nervous because they have no relaxing effects.
3. **T / F**　It is well worth exploring the fantastic world of jazz for music lovers.

### ジャズの人気楽器　サキソフォン

サキソフォンは，1840年代にベルギーの楽器製作者アドルフ・サックスによって開発された楽器です。ジャズでは，トランペット，クラリネット，ベース，ピアノ，ドラムなどとともにサキソフォンは人気の楽器です。チャーリー・パーカー，ジョン・コルトレーン，コールマン・ホーキンズなど優れたサキソフォン奏者が数多くいます。サキソフォンはジャズを象徴する楽器とも言われています。

# Writing

## Exercise 1　日本語に合うように（　　）内に適切な語を書き入れましょう。

1. The United States is (　　　　　) (　　　　　) (　　　　　) jazz was created.
（アメリカはジャズが作られた国です。）

2. Just go to the jazz festival, (　　　　　) (　　　　　) (　　　　　) enjoy fantastic performance.
（ジャズフェスティバルに行ってごらんなさい。そうすれば素晴らしい演奏を楽しむことができます。）

3. Mary started singing (　　　　　) (　　　　　) the music in the contest.
（メアリーはコンテストで音楽に合わせて歌いだした。）

## Exercise 2　（　　）内の語を並べかえて英文を完成させましょう。

1. We found a showcase ( there / which / records / in / many / were / jazz ) in the museum.
（私たちは博物館でたくさんのジャズのレコードが入っている陳列ケースを見つけた。）

2. Jazz can ( mood / create / a / help / relaxed ).

3. There is ( going / piano / nothing / a / recital / like / to ).

## Exercise 3　本文にある表現を用いて，日本語に合うように英文を完成させましょう。

1. 私はパイプオルガンがその教会の内部で演奏されているのを聞いた。

2. あなたはそのギターの演奏にうっとりしてしまうでしょう。

3. 生演奏を聞くことができるのは素晴らしい経験かもしれません。

# Unit 11

# Mercy Killing

## 安楽死

## Listening

### Warm Up

52

**◆ 英語のリズム ◆**

英語らしさを身につけるためにはリズムが重要になります。その練習法として，リズムに乗せて音読するチャンツがあります。英語を話す際は，自然と短縮形になったり，音が繋がったりしますので，チャンツを利用して，英語のフレーズや発音を繰り返し練習してみましょう。

I wish I had a horse.
I wish I had a horse of my own.
And if I had a horse of my own,
That horse would never be lonely.　　（英詩“The Horse March”の冒頭部分）

・手拍子を取りながらリズム感覚を身につけましょう。

**Exercise 1**　音声を聞いて，何の説明かその名前を日本語で（　　）内に書き入れましょう。　53

A（　　　　　　　　）　B（　　　　　　　　）　C（　　　　　　　　）

**Exercise 2**　音声を聞いて，最も適切な応答を一つ選びましょう。　54

1. (A)　(B)　(C)　　2. (A)　(B)　(C)　　3. (A)　(B)　(C)　　4. (A)　(B)　(C)

**Exercise 3**　Opening Conversation を聞いて，下の質問に答えましょう。　55

1. 安楽死を最初に法制化した国はどこか。

________________________________________

2. 森鴎外が安楽死のことを書いた小説は何か。

________________________________________

# Reading

▶ 英文を読んで質問に答えましょう。

56

Shobei and Kisuke were on a small boat sailing down the river. It was a routine job for Shobei to take criminals to a certain place. Shobei found something strange about Kisuke. Shobei knew most criminals got down or felt depressed after killing people. Kisuke, however, looked relieved or even happy. Kisuke explained he was happy because he had helped his sick brother end his own life by removing a razor his brother had inserted in his neck.

This story, *Takase Bune*, written in 1916 by novelist and doctor, Mori Ogai, highlighted and unveiled the underlying issue of euthanasia in our society. *Takase Bune* was the first novel on this subject to attract public attention in Japan. Kisuke's behavior would probably be assumed to be a mercy killing because he saved his brother from a severe pain.

Doctors should not help their patients die, even if there is no chance of recovery from their incurable disease. Recently, two doctors were arrested on suspicion of murdering a Kyoto woman. The woman was an ALS patient and had asked the two doctors to give her a lethal dose of a drug in order to kill her. She chose not natural death but euthanasia by herself. One doctor insisted, "Euthanasia should be tolerated" in his blog. It is, however, illegal in Japan, no matter how much a patient desires.

No matter how many limits we set, some ethical problems remain. More debates or discussion are necessary about euthanasia and the legal power of a living will, which gives instructions regarding our medical treatment if we are unable to do so ourselves. We should also take patients' suffering and the emotional burden of their families into consideration. The point is to value individual patients and let them meet death with peace and dignity. As our society ages, this problem will become increasingly serious.

(309 Words)

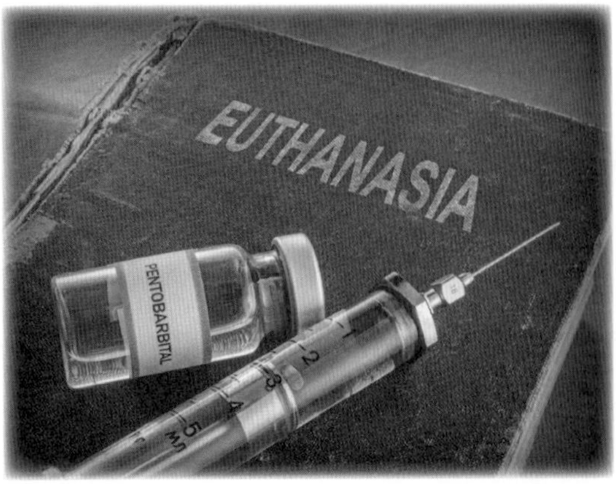


Shobei　庄兵衛（護送役の役人）
Kisuke　喜助（罪人）
*Takase Bune*　高瀬舟
ALS (Amyotrophic Lateral Sclerosis)
　筋萎縮性側索硬化症

## Exercise 1 本文を読んで下の質問に答えましょう。

1. Which of the following statements about Kisuke is true?
   (A) He saved his brother's life by pulling out a razor from his neck.
   (B) His behavior to his brother would be regarded as a mercy killing.
   (C) He really hated his brother and killed him with a razor.
   (D) He got depressed after killing his brother.

2. Which of the following statements is NOT true?
   (A) *Takase Bune* was written in 1916 by Mori Ogai.
   (B) Mori Ogai showed the issue of euthanasia in his novel.
   (C) People showed no interest in the novel, *Takase Bune*.
   (D) Kisuke's brother was freed from a severe pain.

3. Which of the following statements is true?
   (A) A doctor who blogs insisted that euthanasia was protected by law.
   (B) A Kyoto woman committed suicide by taking a lethal dose of a drug on her own.
   (C) A Kyoto woman was an ALS patient and chose death by her own will.
   (D) A Kyoto woman asked the two doctors to cure her of her disease.

## Exercise 2 次の各文が本文の内容に合っていれば **T** を，合っていなければ **F** を選びましょう。

1. **T / F** Kisuke pulled out the razor from his brother's neck in order to kill him on purpose.
2. **T / F** The two doctors were suspected of allowing an ALS patient to die by giving her a lethal dose of a drug.
3. **T / F** When patients are in a hopeless condition, we should never take the burden of the family into account.

### 安楽死

安楽死とは死が切迫した不治の患者を苦しみから解放するために死なせることを指します。医学，法学，倫理学などの分野で議論が分かれる問題で，現在，ほとんどの国で違法です。ヨーロッパの一部の国やアメリカの一部の州では法律により認めているところもありますが，日本では法制化されていません。社会の高齢化に伴って，ますますこの問題を議論する重要性が高まっています。

# Writing

## Exercise 1　日本語に合うように（　　）内に適切な語を書き入れましょう。

1. Mike (　　　　　　) (　　　　　　) when he heard that the operation was successful.
（マイクは手術が成功したと聞いてほっとしたようだった。）

2. The patient had (　　　　　　) (　　　　　　) (　　　　　　) recovery from his serious illness.
（その患者は重病から回復する見込みが全くなかった。）

3. The old woman (　　　　　　) her doctors (　　　　　　) (　　　　　　) give her unnecessary treatment.
（老婦人は医師団に不必要な治療をしないように頼んだ。）

## Exercise 2　（　　）内の語を並べかえて英文を完成させましょう。

1. It is a duty ( to / for / care / of / take / children ) their parents.
（両親の世話をするのは子どもの義務です。）

2. The train accident was ( by / caused / to / assumed / be ) heavy snow.

3. I ( the / will / you / results / let / later / know ).

## Exercise 3　本文にある表現を用いて，日本語に合うように英文を完成させましょう。

1. 彼は１台ではなく２台のスマートフォンを所有しています。

2. 何が起ころうとも，私はいつもあなたを愛します。

3. 私たちは彼女の希望を考慮に入れました。

# Unit 12

# Online Communication

オンラインでコミュニケーション

## Listening

### Warm Up

57

**◆ イントネーション ◆**

イントネーションは主にだんだんと下げる下降調，だんだんと上げる上昇調，下げてから上げる下降上昇調の 3 つのパターンがあります。音の高低変化によって意味や感情の違いを表します。これらの 3 つの変化を意識して発音しましょう。

Where are you going?　下降調（通常 Wh 疑問文は下降調を用いられる）
A: Have you ever been to London?　上昇調（Yes-No 疑問文）
B: Yes.　下降上昇調　含みのある曖昧な返事

A: What day does David come to school next?　下降調
B: I think he said Monday.　上昇調

**Exercise 1**　音声を聞いて，何の説明か，その名前を日本語で（　　）内に書き入れましょう。　58

A（　　　　　　　　　）　B（　　　　　　　　　）　C（　　　　　　　　　）

**Exercise 2**　音声を聞いて，最も適切な応答を一つ選びましょう。　59

1. (A)　(B)　(C)　　2. (A)　(B)　(C)　　3. (A)　(B)　(C)　　4. (A)　(B)　(C)

**Exercise 3**　Opening Conversation を聞いて，下の質問に答えましょう。　60

1. Bob はどうしてうれしそうにしているのか。

______________________________

2. オンラインミーティングの時，カメラから離れて座っている人の何が分かりにくいのか。

______________________________

# Reading

▶ 英文を読んで質問に答えましょう。

61

Virtual meetings are now part of everyday life thanks to the emergence of COVID-19. While most people are used to text messaging, video calls with friends and family, and connecting through social media, the term "online communication" took on a whole new meaning in 2020.

People were suddenly forced to work or study from home. Many who had never before heard of Zoom, Microsoft Teams, or Google Meet, were now thrust in front of web-cams, sharing screens and struggling to connect with those on the other side of the monitor. Effective and engaging communication is in itself a challenge, but it is now further complicated by the distance and feeling of isolation that separates the messenger from their audience.

The good news is that there are small, practical things we can all do to make us better online communicators. This means taking the necessary steps to help us feel more comfortable and confident, both as online meeting presenters and participants.

The first step is to ensure that you are equipped and set up for your online meeting. Taking the time to check your internet connection, testing your speakers (or headphones), microphone and camera will help everything go smoothly. Make sure that your camera is at eye level and that there is enough light for your face to be seen.

Another point to keep in mind is the importance of non-verbal communication, especially if the number of people attending is limited. You can let the presenter know that you are actively listening by paying more attention to your facial expression, nodding your head, or gesturing your hands. You can even send messages through the chat or use the "react" functions included in most online meeting platforms.

Online communication can be stressful. However, it can also be a fun, convenient, and interesting way to connect with people, if we are respectful of others and make the effort to master the technology that helps bring the world together.

(326 Words)

## Exercise 1 本文を読んで下の質問に答えましょう。

1. Which of the following statements about online communication is true?
   (A) It is useful only for those who are used to text messaging.
   (B) It is nice to communicate with people from all over the world, who live far away.
   (C) Zoom, Microsoft Teams, and Google Meet were popular platforms.
   (D) It is good to lose contact with people around you.

2. What devices do we need for virtual meetings?
   (A) web-cameras
   (B) internet connection
   (C) microphones
   (D) All of the above

3. Which of the following is NOT true?
   (A) Paying attention to gestures and facial expressions is important.
   (B) You can send and receive messages using the chat features on various platforms.
   (C) You don't have to set your web-camera at eye level online.
   (D) Online communication will go smoothly if certain steps are observed.

## Exercise 2 次の各文が本文の内容に合っていれば **T** を，合っていなければ **F** を選びましょう。

1. **T / F** "Online communication" was a new word used to describe social media in 2020.
2. **T / F** Our facial expressions and gestures will let both online presenters and participants know that we are active listeners.
3. **T / F** If you master good manners and information technology, you can be an engaging communicator.

### オンラインによるコミュニケーション

コロナウイルスが蔓延した影響で，オンラインによるコミュニケーションの機会が格段に増えました。オンライン会議，オンライン授業，オンライン飲み会など今まで耳にすることがほとんどなかった言葉を日常的に使うようになりました。パソコンやプラットフォームの操作にとまどった人も多かったと思います。時代の変化に合わせ，今までのコミュニケーションのあり方を検証するチャンスかも知れません。

# Writing

## Exercise 1 日本語に合うように（　　）内に適切な語を書き入れましょう。

1. Many people are (　　　　) (　　　　) (　　　　) to social media.
（多くの人はソーシャルメディアに接続することに慣れています。）

2. For (　　　　) information, please check our website.
（詳しくは，ウエブサイトをご覧ください。）

3. The first point to (　　　　) (　　　　) (　　　　) is to make eye contact.
（最初に心に留めておくべきポイントはアイコンタクトをとることです。）

## Exercise 2 （　　）内の語を並べかえて英文を完成させましょう。

1. We ( forced / of / online / study / because / were / to ) the spread of the virus.
（ウイルスがまん延したために，オンラインでの勉強を強いられました。）

______________________________

2. The committee had ( sharing / an / meeting, / screens / online ).

______________________________

3. Online communication ( to / interesting / can / connect / be / an / way ) with people.

______________________________

## Exercise 3 本文にある表現を用いて，日本語に合うように英文を完成させましょう。

1. リラックスするための時間をとることは重要です。

______________________________

2. そのファイルを必ずあなたのコンピュータに保存しなさい。

______________________________

3. 彼女の顔の表情や身振りに注意を払いなさい。

______________________________

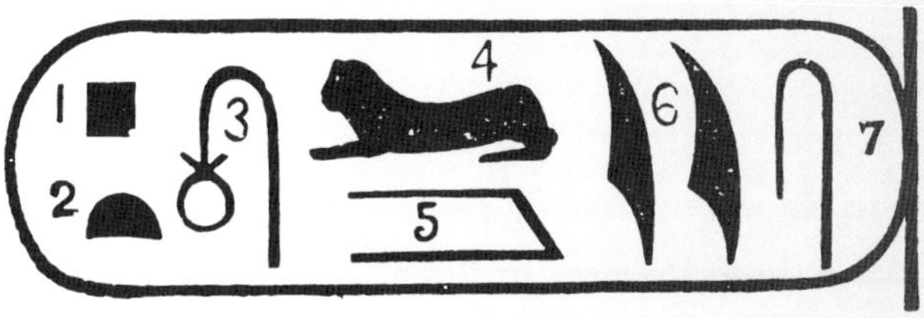


# Unit 13

# The Secret of the Rosetta Stone ヒエログリフ解読の鍵

## Listening

### Warm Up

62

**◆ 外来語と英語の違い ◆**

日本語はほぼ全ての音節に母音 [a][i][u][e][o] が入りますが，英語は母音が入らず子音が連続する単語が多くあります。日本人は母語の影響で，英語の発音の際に余分な母音を挿入してしまう傾向があります。日本語の中の外来語になっているものについては特に注意しましょう。

| | | | |
|---|---|---|---|
| beer<br>ビール | smartphone<br>スマートフォン | drink<br>ドリンク | allergy<br>アレルギー |
| juice<br>ジュース | towel<br>タオル | bed<br>ベッド | chocolate<br>チョコレート |

**Exercise 1** 音声を聞いて，何のアイテムの説明か日本語で（　　）内に書き入れましょう。 63

A（　　　　　　　　　）　B（　　　　　　　　　）　C（　　　　　　　　　）

**Exercise 2** 音声を聞いて，最も適切な応答を一つ選びましょう。 64

1. (A)　(B)　(C)　　2. (A)　(B)　(C)　　3. (A)　(B)　(C)　　4. (A)　(B)　(C)

**Exercise 3** Opening Conversation を聞いて，下の質問に答えましょう。 65

1. David は「雅」という名前は雅に合っていると言ったのか。

_______________________________________________

2. 雅は，片仮名や平仮名は英語の発音の仕組みと同じと言っているのか。

_______________________________________________

▶ 英文を読んで質問に答えましょう。

66

The Rosetta Stone was found at the construction site of Fort Julian in 1799. Purely by accident, a young soldier in Napoleon's army noticed the stone sticking out of the wall. It was named after the town Rosetta in Egypt. The Rosetta Stone was like a messenger whose mission was to open the door to ancient Egyptian civilization. The messages were written in hieroglyphics, demotic, and Greek.

It was assumed that these messages were of great importance because the inscriptions on the stone were actually based on a single text written in three different scripts. The Greek writing was soon decoded by some scholars, and the demotic portion was interpreted soon after. But the hieroglyphic text was very difficult. Even though images of this kind had been found throughout the whole area of the Nile valley, nobody had yet been able to read them.

When you piece together jigsaw puzzles, do sudoku, or play the game of *go*, you may sometimes get stuck and feel frustrated. If you make a wrong move, you may end up going around in circles. Similarly, it seemed at the time as though the key to reading the hieroglyphics was nowhere to be found. It was J. F. Champollion that made a breakthrough in deciphering the hieroglyphics. He was a French linguist and was well-versed in the Coptic.

At the initial stage of his investigation, Champollion couldn't find the key to unlocking the code. Suddenly, Champollion had a flash of genius, an idea that would allow almost full deciphering of the hieroglyphics. By comparing the hieroglyphics with other separate references, he found two royal names, *Ptolemy* and *Cleopatra*. Champollion was sure at least some of the hieroglyphics were letters, not just pictures. This was the beginning of a dramatic discovery.

Now, thanks to his excellent work, we can travel back to the mysterious land of ancient Egypt. If you visit the Egyptian section of the British Museum in London, you will be able to see the artifact that made this all possible: The Rosetta Stone.

(340 Words)

the Nile valley　ナイル川流域
Ptolemy　プトレマイオス
Cleopatra　クレオパトラ

## Exercise 1 本文を読んで下の質問に答えましょう。

1. Where did the name Rosetta Stone originate from?
   (A) It came from the name of the wall found at Fort Julian.
   (B) It originated from the construction site of Fort Julian.
   (C) It came from the messages written on the stone.
   (D) It originated from the name of the town Rosetta.

2. Why was the Rosetta Stone so important?
   (A) Because very important messages were written on the Rosetta Stone.
   (B) Because the hieroglyphic texts seemed very difficult to decipher.
   (C) Because all three different scripts presented the same content.
   (D) Because similar picture writings were found throughout the Nile Valley.

3. What was the event that led to the decoding of the hieroglyphic text?
   (A) Champollion was a genius for deciphering the hieroglyphic texts.
   (B) Champollion discovered two names in the hieroglyphic texts.
   (C) Champollion had the idea that the hieroglyphics were just pictures.
   (D) Champollion made a major discovery that allowed him to read Coptic.

## Exercise 2 次の各文が本文の内容に合っていれば **T** を，合っていなければ **F** を選びましょう。

1. **T / F** Three different scripts were written on the Rosetta Stone. They were three unique texts that were related.
2. **T / F** The hieroglyphics were recognized only as mere pictures, so the key to reading them was nowhere to be found.
3. **T / F** Champollion was successful in deciphering the hieroglyphics by finding two names of Egyptian royal family members.

### ロゼッタストーンの奇跡

ロゼッタストーンに書かれていたことは，当時のエジプト王の業績を称賛する内容で，特別なものではありませんでした。ところが，同じ内容が3種類の言語で書かれていたことで，一気に注目されました。誰も読むことができなかったヒエログリフ（象形文字）の解読にシャンポリオンが成功したことで，エジプト研究が飛躍的に発展しました。ロゼッタストーンは，現在ロンドンの大英博物館のエジプト室で展示されています。

# Writing

**Exercise 1** 日本語に合うように（　）内に適切な語を書き入れましょう。

1. Sayaka was (　　　　　　) (　　　　　　) a famous film actress.
（さやかはある有名な映画女優にちなんで名付けられた。）

2. The information was (　　　　　　) (　　　　　　) (　　　　　　) to linguists.
（この情報は言語学者にとってとても重要だった。）

3. If you can't find the correct answer, you may (　　　　　　) (　　　　　　).
（もし正しい答えを見つけられなければ，行き詰まってしまうかもしれない。）

**Exercise 2** （　）内の語を並べかえて英文を完成させましょう。

1. It was ( that / were / writings / these / assumed / written / picture ) in ancient Egypt.
（これらの絵文字は古代エジプトで書かれたと想定された。）

______________________________________________

2. It seemed ( to / though / the key / breaking / as ) the code was nowhere.

______________________________________________

3. It was Sherlock Holmes ( important / solve / an / clue / that / got / to ) the case.

______________________________________________

**Exercise 3** 本文にある表現を用いて，日本語に合うように英文を完成させましょう。

1. メッセージは３種類の異なった文字で書かれていた。

______________________________________________

2. もし間違った方向に行けば，堂々巡りになるかもしれません。

______________________________________________

3. 彼の優れた業績のおかげで，エジプトの象形文字の読み書きができます。

______________________________________________

# Unit 14

# Neuvola

## フィンランドの子育てモデル

## Listening

### Warm Up

67

**◆ アメリカ英語の特徴 ◆**

英語の中でもアメリカ英語とイギリス英語では同じ単語でも音色の違いがあります。例えば，母音のあとの r 音は，アメリカ英語では明確に発音されます。

アメリカ英語

| | |
|---|---|
| wat**er**, ov**er**<br>(ウォーラー) | 母音のあとの [r] を響かせて発音する |
| **pepp**er, **t**ake | 日本語のパ行やタ行の音よりも強い呼気で発音する |
| **sche**dule [**sk**édʒu:l]<br>(スケジュール) | 語頭の音は [ske] と発音する |

**Exercise 1** 音声を聞いて，何の説明か，その名前を日本語で（　　）内に書き入れましょう。 68

A（　　　　　　　　　）　B（　　　　　　　　　）　C（　　　　　　　　　）

**Exercise 2** 音声を聞いて，最も適切な応答を一つ選びましょう。 69

1. (A)　(B)　(C)　　2. (A)　(B)　(C)　　3. (A)　(B)　(C)　　4. (A)　(B)　(C)

**Exercise 3** Opening Conversation を聞いて，下の質問に答えましょう。 70

1. 雅は Elias を待っている間に何をしていたのか。

______________________________________________

2. 雅と Elias は何が大変だと言っているのか。

______________________________________________

# Reading

▶ 英文を読んで質問に答えましょう。

71

Neuvola is a place that provides services to people during pregnancy or while raising children in Finland. The term is a Finnish word made up of two parts: *neuvo* (advice) and *-la* (a suffix meaning a "place").

Neuvola originated in the early 20th century when Finland had high maternal and infant mortality rates because of poverty. In 1904, the first place for distributing sterilized milk was established in Helsinki. The child-welfare movement became important in the 1920s, while Finland was recovering from the civil war following its independence from Russia in 1917. Groups of doctors, nurses, and midwives took the initiative in providing check-ups and advice on nutrition and hygiene for expectant mothers. They also supplied childcare packages including baby clothes to support families financially. Having officially been institutionalized in 1944, Neuvola is now located in every municipality, with 99.8% of parents and children using its facilities.

Neuvola is highly regarded for its continuous childcare support. People are assigned to the same public health nurses until their children reach the age of six. Neuvola nurses offer check-ups through pregnancy, health checks for infants, counseling, home visits, and links to other specialist services. The Finnish government grants €140 or gives a childcare package to every pregnant woman. All forms of support, including hospital fees for childbirth, are free of charge, regardless of nationality and family status. Finland also provides free or heavily subsidized day-care services for all children, irrespective of whether or not their parents work. The country has built a support system that is widely accessible and available to all.

The Japanese government has developed its own childcare policies based on the Finnish model. Each municipality has comprehensive support centers for families with children and has increased services to take care of infants. Families use daycare centers, kindergartens, or other facilities free of charge or with much-reduced fees. However, it may still take time and effort for Japan to create comfortable spaces broadly accessible to everybody.

(326 Words)

## ***Exercise 1*** 本文を読んで下の質問に答えましょう。

1. What is Neuvola?
   (A) It is a kind of school where young children start to learn.
   (B) It is a service Russia introduced in Finland in the early 20th century.
   (C) It is a center where young people go to get some financial advice.
   (D) It is a facility that provides support for families with young children.

2. Why has Finland developed Neuvola?
   (A) There were many doctors, nurses, and midwives.
   (B) A lot of children and mothers died without any support.
   (C) Many people started to have smaller families in urban areas.
   (D) They could receive huge financial support from Russia.

3. What kind of support can people receive in Finland?
   (A) They can get specialist advice continuously for raising a child.
   (B) They can get free meal tickets every time they visit Neuvola.
   (C) Every child can have a math tutor visiting home periodically.
   (D) Hospital fees for all generations are free of charge.

## ***Exercise 2*** 次の各文が本文の内容に合っていれば **T** を，合っていなければ **F** を選びましょう。

1. **T / F** In Finland, almost all households with small children visit Neuvola offices.
2. **T / F** In Finland, children cannot go to day care when their parents work at home.
3. **T / F** Nowadays, Japan also has a perfect childcare support system like Finland.

### フィンランド語

フィンランド語は格変化の多い言語として知られています。膠着語と呼ばれ，接尾辞を重ねていくことで単語に意味を継ぎ足していきます。英語の “in ...”（～の中で／に）にあたる内格は，基本的に “-ssa/ssä” をつけることで表されます。“Minä asun Helsingissä.”（私はヘルシンキに住んでいます。）という表現は，“Ibarakissa,” “Osakassa,” “Japanissa” と，日本の地名を並べて使うこともできます。童謡の「あんたがたどこさ」みたいでしょう？

## Writing

**Exercise 1** 日本語に合うように（　　）内に適切な語を書き入れましょう。

1. I was born in the 2000s (　　　　　) my parents lived in Finland.
（両親がフィンランドで暮らしていた2000年代に私は生まれました。）

2. Elias learned to skate even at the (　　　　　) (　　　　　) three.
（エリアスは3歳の時にはスケートができるようになりました。）

3. The UN convention affirms that every (　　　　　) (　　　　　) a right to education.
（国連条約はあらゆる子どもが教育を受ける権利を認めている。）

**Exercise 2** （　　）内の語を並べかえて英文を完成させましょう。

1. You may want to ( to / sauna / visiting / while / try /going ) Finland.
（フィンランド滞在中には，サウナに行ってみるのも良いかもしれません。）

______________________________________________

2. During adolescence, teenagers ( seek / from / often / to / independence / gain ) parents.

______________________________________________

3. Inclusive education is the idea to educate ( together, / differences / of / all / their / regardless / children ).

______________________________________________

**Exercise 3** 本文にある表現を用いて，日本語に合うように英文を完成させましょう。

1. 私たちのグループは，教育に関心のある学生で構成されています。

______________________________________________

2. 日本では，子どもは無償で医療を受けることができます。

______________________________________________

3. 電車には，妊婦や小さな子どもを連れている乗客のための優先席があります。

______________________________________________

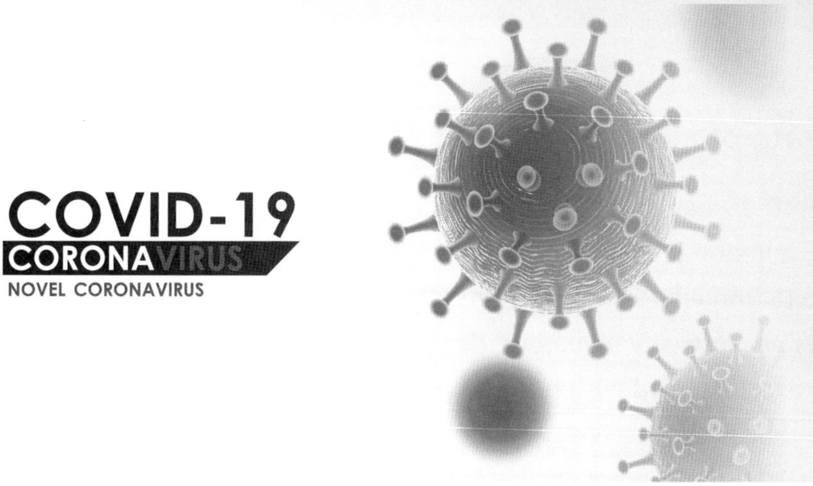


# Unit 15

# COVID-19

コロナウイルス禍

## Listening

### Warm Up

72

**◆ イギリス英語の特徴 ◆**

イギリス英語は，母音のあとの r の音を落として（ほとんど聞こえない）発音されます。また，子音では [p], [t], [k] のような無声破裂音がイギリス英語ではアメリカ英語よりも強く発音される傾向があります。

イギリス英語

water, over　　母音は短く，そのあとの [r] の音を落として発音する
（ウォッタ）

pepper, take　　アメリカ英語よりもさらに強い呼気で発音する

schedule [ʃédju:l]　　語頭の音は [ʃe] と発音する
（シェジュール）

**Exercise 1** 音声を聞いて，ウイルス関連の何の説明か，その名前を日本語で（　　）内に書き入れましょう。

73

A（　　　　　　　　）　B（　　　　　　　　）　C（　　　　　　　　）

**Exercise 2** 音声を聞いて，最も適切な応答を一つ選びましょう。

74

1. (A)　(B)　(C)　　2. (A)　(B)　(C)　　3. (A)　(B)　(C)　　4. (A)　(B)　(C)

**Exercise 3** Opening Conversation を聞いて，下の質問に答えましょう。

75

1. 美穂の父親はなぜ入院しているのか。

______________________________

2. アメリカにいる Bob の友達は日本で何を習いたいと思っているのか。

______________________________

# Reading

▶ 英文を読んで質問に答えましょう。

76

The onset of COVID-19 has thrown the world as we know it into utter chaos. It seems like no one can stop it and no one can tell what will happen next, with scientists still unable to find effective ways to prevent infection against the newly mutated strains. At its peak, streets in major cities all across the globe were empty, while hospitals were overwhelmed with infected patients.

It is no wonder that everyone is scared of this new, invisible enemy. Many have compared COVID-19 to the more familiar influenza, but make no mistake: this virus is far more fatal, contagious, and hard to detect. While some people can be infected and exhibit few or no symptoms, they can still act as carriers and make other people sick. This combination is what makes this disease so dangerous.

Some pharmaceutical companies have developed COVID-19 vaccines known as mRNA vaccines, using revolutionary technology. The Japanese government recommends the vaccines manufactured by Pfizer and Moderna. Medical workers and those at greater risk of complications from the virus, including the elderly, are prioritized. The problem of mutation, however, makes a planned immunization program impractical.

The spread of the virus changed our lives and society dramatically. A great number of companies have switched to doing business online, allowing employees to work remotely. Most schools had to cancel on-campus events, while universities were forced to conduct classes using virtual learning platforms. On the other hand, there are also little changes we can easily practice every day, such as wearing masks, washing hands, social distancing, and other basic sanitary habits.

Though the future is filled with uncertainty, that doesn't mean that all hope is lost. If there was ever a time to appreciate the blessings we so often take for granted, such as our health, the love of family and friends, the freedom to work, study, and travel, now is that time. The key is to strike that balance between staying calm and positive, and exercising caution in service of personal and public safety.

(340 Words)

## *Exercise 1* 本文を読んで下の質問に答えましょう。

1. Which is true about the spread of COVID-19?
   (A) Everyone can guess what will happen in the future.
   (B) Streets in major cities are crowded with many people.
   (C) Scientists have been successful in preventing infection.
   (D) Hospitals are full of coronavirus patients.

2. Why is this virus strain so dangerous?
   (A) Because the infected patients will become more serious.
   (B) Because people often are not aware they are infected.
   (C) Because it is as deadly an illness as the influenza virus.
   (D) Because people are not so scared of this invisible enemy.

3. What does the outbreak of the virus change in our daily lives?
   (A) People are beginning to give up keeping their basic sanitary habits.
   (B) Many office workers are required by employers to work at their office.
   (C) We are always wearing masks and keeping our distance in crowded places.
   (D) We are free to work, study, and travel, wherever and whenever we want to.

## *Exercise 2* 次の各文が本文の内容に合っていれば **T** を，合っていなければ **F** を選びましょう。

1. **T / F** We have witnessed in real time this virus turn into a pandemic.
2. **T / F** A vaccine against COVID-19 has not yet been developed.
3. **T / F** It is important for us to keep ourselves and the people around us safe.

### 新型コロナウイルス

人類は今までに経験したことがない新型コロナウイルスの脅威にさらされています。ウイルスは変異しながら繰り返し襲ってきます。感染者数は急激に増加したり，減少したりしています。私たちは驚異的な速さでワクチンを開発し，ウイルスに対抗していますが，世界中で猛威をふるうウイルスが終息する兆しが見えません。現在，オミクロン株が出現し，まだ先が見通せない状態が続いています。

# Writing

**Exercise 1** 日本語に合うように（　　）内に適切な語を書き入れましょう。

1. Scientists try to find effective ways (　　　　　　) (　　　　　　) infection against the virus.
   （科学者たちはウイルスの感染を防ぐ効果的な方法を見つけようとしている。）

2. The elderly are at (　　　　　　) (　　　　　　) (　　　　　　) complications from the virus.
   （年配の人はウイルスの合併症にかかるリスクが高い。）

3. We took (　　　　　　) (　　　　　　) that university students enjoy their happy campus life.
   （大学生が楽しいキャンパスライフを楽しむのは当然だと思っていた。）

**Exercise 2** （　　）内の語を並べかえて英文を完成させましょう。

1. It is ( wonder / scared / that / is / of / no / everyone ) COVID-19.
   （誰もが COVID-19 を怖がるのは不思議なことではない。）

   ______________________________________________

2. Some infected people ( act / carriers / as / still / can ) even if they have no symptoms.

   ______________________________________________

3. The COVID-19 vaccines ( pharmaceutical / by / been / companies / developed / some / have ).

   ______________________________________________

**Exercise 3** 本文にある表現を用いて，日本語に合うように英文を完成させましょう。

1. 病院は COVID-19 の患者であふれている。

   ______________________________________________

2. 多くの大学はオンライン授業に切り替えた。

   ______________________________________________

3. COVID-19 のまん延で，すべて希望がなくなったという訳ではない。

   ______________________________________________

# 付　録　①

**【機能語と内容語】**

強アクセントと弱アクセントは品詞の違いにあります。強く発音される品詞と弱く発音される品詞について以下の表に整理しておきます。

| 内容語＝強アクセント | | 機能語＝弱アクセント | |
|---|---|---|---|
| 品詞 | 例 | 品詞 | 例 |
| 一般動詞 | go, do, study, listen | be 動詞 | is, am, are |
| 名詞 | Nagoya, Mary, flower, house | 人称代名詞 | I, you, he, she, we, they |
| 形容詞 | red, small, good, difficult | 助動詞 | do, can, may, must, should |
| 副詞 | yesterday, now, slowly | 前置詞 | to, in, on, at, for, with |
| 疑問詞 | what, when, where, why, how | 冠詞 | a, an, the |
| 指示詞 | this, that | 接続詞 | and, but, that |
| 数詞 | one, two, three | 関係詞 | that, who, which |

# 付録 ②

**【弱形】**

**付録①**で確認したように，弱形で発音される英単語は一般的に機能語です。機能語は文法的な機能としては重要ですが，意味的には重要視されないため，文中では不明瞭に発音されます。下記の弱形の発音記号では，曖昧な母音 [ə] が多く入っているのが分かりますね。モデル音声を聞き，弱形を意識して例文の練習をしてみましょう。

| 単語 | 強形 | 弱形 |
|---|---|---|
| the | ði | ðə ðɪ ði |
| and | ænd | n̩ ən ənd |
| his | hɪz | ɪz |
| her | hɜː | ə |
| your | jɔː | jə |
| he | hiː | hɪ hi ɪ i |
| she | ʃiː | ʃɪ ʃi |
| him | hɪm | ɪm |
| for | fɔː(r) | fə(r) |
| of | ɒv | əv |
| have | hæv | əv |
| has | hæz | əz |
| to | tuː | tə |

77

1. Is this for me? [fə(r)]
2. I'm thinking of you. [əv]
3. David will go to college in the afternoon. [tə], [ði]
4. She has a nice umbrella. [əz], [ə]
5. Miyabi and Gerald are watching Asian dramas. [ən], [ər]

# 付　録　③

## 【母音の口の形】

英語の母音は，日本語の母音と比較する縦にも横にも広げて発音します。写真を見て，前から見た口の形（縦横の大きさ）に注目し，鏡を見ながら口の形を真似して練習してみましょう。

### 日英の母音「イ」と「ウ」の違い

| 緊張母音の「イ」の形<br>口を横に引っ張って「イー」 | 弛緩母音の「イ」の形<br>口を少し縦に開けて「イ」 | 日本語の「イ」の形 |
|---|---|---|
|  |  | 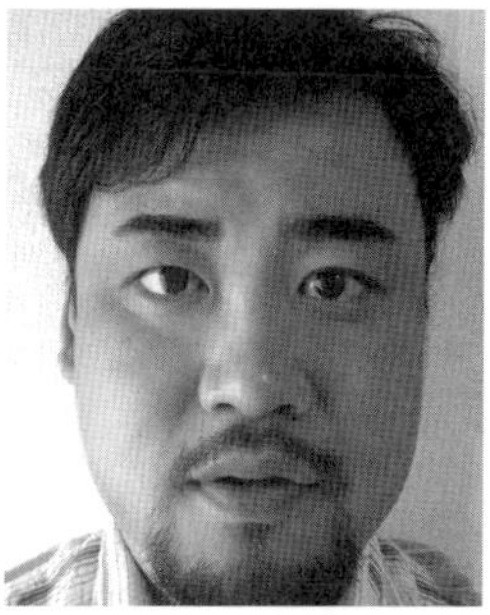 |

| 緊張母音の「ウ」の形<br>唇をすぼめて「ウー」 | 弛緩母音の「ウ」の形<br>あまり力を入れずに「ウ」 | 日本語の「ウ」の形 |
|---|---|---|
| 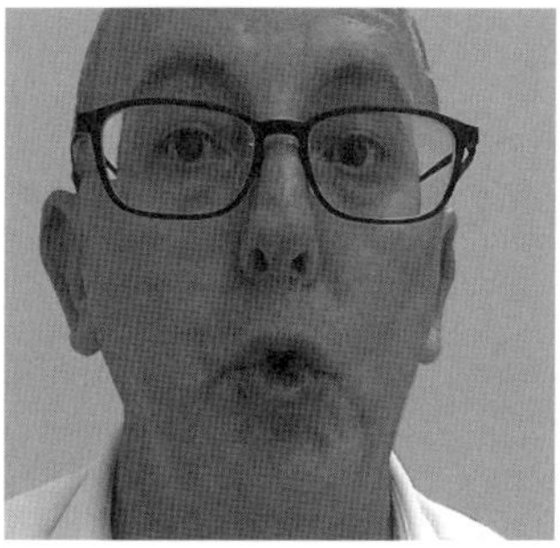 |  |  |

# 付　録　④

**【詩の韻律】**

『ロミオとジュリエット』のセリフ

**ジュリエット**

| | |
|---|---|
| ああ，ロミオ，ロミオ， | O Romeo, Romeo! |
| どうしてあなたはロミオなの。 | Wherefore art thou Romeo? |
| | |
| 名前がなんだというの？ | What’s in a name? |
| バラと呼ばれるあの花は， | That which we call a rose |
| ほかの名前で呼ぼうとも， | By any other word would smell as sweet |
| 甘い香りは変わらない。 | |

# Vocabulary Focus / Grammar Points

## Unit 1　College Education

### *Reading Section*

### *Vocabulary Focus*

| | | | |
|---|---|---|---|
| L.4 | higher education　高等教育 | L.4-5 | practical learning　実学 |
| L.5 | fields of study　研究分野 | L.6 | business administration　経営学 |
| L.6 | applied science　応用科学 | L.8 | curricula　カリキュラム |
| L.9-10 | specialized knowledge　専門知識 | L.12 | Bologne　ボローニャ |
| L.15 | discipline　教義，規律 | L.16 | the seven liberal arts　自由学芸七科 |
| L.16 | rhetoric　修辞 | L.16 | arithmetic　算術 |
| L.16 | geometry　幾何 | L.16 | astronomy　天文 |
| L.18-19 | civic life　市民生活 | L.19 | hence　それ故に，従って |
| L.20 | theology　神学 | L.21 | the Meiji Restoration　明治維新 |
| L.23 | prioritize　優先させる | L.24 | enlightenment　明確な理解 |
| L.24-25 | organization of academic departments　学部編制 | | |

### *Grammar Points*

分詞修飾／受動態／コロンの用法

## Unit 2　3D Ashura

### *Reading Section*

### *Vocabulary Focus*

| | | | |
|---|---|---|---|
| L.1 | entertainment facility　娯楽施設 | L.5 | repeat customer　リピーター |
| L.7 | spectacular firework　壮観な花火 | L.11 | Cinderella Castle　シンデレラ城 |
| L.15 | venue　（イベントなどの）開催場所 | L.19 | Buddhist image　仏像 |
| L.20 | merciful look　慈悲深いまなざし | L.21 | enchant　魅了する |
| L.24 | cutting-edge technology　最先端技術 | L.25 | pop-up　浮き上がる |
| L.25 | replica　レプリカ | | |

### *Grammar Points*

関係代名詞（非制限用法）／関係代名詞 what ／完了不定詞

## Unit 3　Korean and Chinese Dramas

### *Reading Section*

### *Vocabulary Focus*

| | | | |
|---|---|---|---|
| L.4 | incorporate　組み込む | L.5 | cuisine　独特の料理 |
| L.8 | weave　織り込む | L.8 | narrative　物語 |
| L.9 | depict　描写する | L.10 | pertinent　関連した |
| L.11 | tailor　仕立てる | L.11 | cultural context　文化的背景 |
| L.12 | Joseon period　朝鮮時代 | L.14 | motif　モチーフ |
| L.14-15 | The Three Kingdom Saga　三国志 | L.15 | gorgeous　とても美しい |
| L.15 | costume　衣装 | L.15 | ornament　装飾品 |
| L.17 | Li Bai　李白 | L.17 | cite　引用する |
| L.17 | quote　引用する | L.18 | prevalent　普及している |
| L.22 | phonetic　音声の | L.24 | triangular　三角形の |
| L.27 | attribute　特性 | | |

### *Grammar Points*

分詞構文（付帯状況）／ if 節／助動詞 may

# Vocabulary Focus / Grammar Points

## Unit 4　Rice Plant

***Reading Section***

***Vocabulary Focus***

| | | | |
|---|---|---|---|
| L.2 | sources of revenue　収入源 | L.2 | sustain　下から支える |
| L.4 | staple food　主食 | L.4 | millennia　千年 |
| L.5 | biotechnological means　バイオ技術 | L.5 | ensure　確実にする |
| L.5 | harvest　収穫 | L.7 | fertility　豊かさ |
| L.8-9 | curry-and-rice　カレーライス | L.9 | delicacy　おいしさ |
| L.10 | plain rice　白いご飯 | L.11 | brew　醸造する |
| L.13 | medieval　中世の | L.13 | bands of samurai warriors　武士団 |
| L.13 | loyalty　忠誠心 | L.14 | natural disaster　自然災害 |
| L.15 | rice ball　おにぎり | L.17 | drought　干ばつ |
| L.17-18 | dry-land rice plant　陸稲 | L.18 | NERICA New Rice for Africa |
| L.21-22 | cold-resistant species　寒さに強い品種 | L.22 | crossing process　交配作業 |
| L.23 | popularity　人気 | | |

***Grammar Points***

現在完了進行形／関係代名詞（非制限用法）／関係副詞（非制限用法）

## Unit 5　A Thousand Years of Love

***Reading Section***

***Vocabulary Focus***

| | | | |
|---|---|---|---|
| L.2 | love affairs　恋愛 | L.2 | Cleopatra　クレオパトラ |
| L.3 | William Shakespeare　ウィリアム・シェイクスピア（1564-1616）　イギリスの劇作家 | | |
| L.6 | suicide　自殺 | L.7 | Yoshitsune　源義経 |
| L.10 | play his flute in reply　横笛で吹き返す | L.11 | overwhelming　圧倒的な |
| L.11 | hardship　困難 | L.12 | puppet show　文楽 |
| L.12 | ningyo-joruri　人形浄瑠璃 | L.13 | heir　継承者 |
| L.13 | clan　一族 | L.14 | tragic　悲劇の |
| L.15 | pursuer　追っ手 | L.16 | re-enact　（歴史上のできごとを）再現する |
| L.17 | Benkei　弁慶 | L.18 | Kanjin-cho　勧進帳 |
| L.18 | kabuki program　歌舞伎の演目 | L.19 | fascinating　魅力的な |
| L.20 | sorrow　深い悲しみ | L.21 | in vain　無駄 |
| L.21 | destiny　運命 | L.25 | Joruri's Abyss　浄瑠璃が淵 |
| L.26 | tomb　墓 | | |

***Grammar Points***

must ＋ have ＋過去分詞／過去分詞（後置修飾）／ It might ~ that

## Unit 6　Coming to America

***Reading Section***

***Vocabulary Focus***

| | | | |
|---|---|---|---|
| L.2 | cherry blossom　桜の花 | L.2 | bloom　花が咲く |
| L.3 | Connecticut　コネティカット州 | L.5 | get used to　慣れる |
| L.6-7 | Victorian house　ヴィクトリア朝様式の家 | L.7 | convert　改装する |
| L.8 | landlord　家主 | L.10 | cozy　居心地のよい |
| L.10 | loads of　たくさんの | L.11 | inconvenient　不便な |
| L.12 | grocery　雑貨店 | L.14 | Nor'easter ＝ Northeaster　北東の暴風 |
| L.16 | now that　なので | L.19 | pricey　値段が高い |
| L.19 | server　給仕する人 | | |

***Grammar Points***

now that ／形式主語 it ／使役動詞 make

# Vocabulary Focus / Grammar Points

## Unit 7　Aqua Blue

***Reading Section***

***Vocabulary Focus***

| | | | |
|---|---|---|---|
| L.1 | take up （趣味などを）始める | L.4 | air tank 空気タンク |
| L.4-5 | atmospheric pressure 気圧 | L.7 | neutral buoyancy 中性浮力 |
| L.7 | training camp 合宿 | L.8 | Miyake-jima Island 三宅島（伊豆七島のひとつ） |
| L.14 | clownfish クマノミ | L.14 | sea anemone イソギンチャク |
| L.16 | paradise 楽園 | L.23 | greenie 環境保護論者 |
| L.24 | Planet Ark オーストラリアの環境保護団体 | L.27 | debris ごみ |

***Grammar Points***

the ＋比較級＋ SV, the ＋比較級＋ SV ／ as if の用法／程度 some

## Unit 8　Roman Numerals

***Reading Section***

***Vocabulary Focus***

| | | | |
|---|---|---|---|
| L.1 | numeral 数字 | L.2 | denote 表示する |
| L.3 | form 筆記体系 | L.4 | Arabic アラビアの |
| L.5 | be accustomed to 慣れる | L.7 | script 筆記 |
| L.7 | utilize 利用する | L.8 | devise 考案する |
| L.10 | Latin ラテン語の | L.11 | employ 使用する |
| L.17 | corresponding value 相当する価値 | L.19 | subtraction 引き算 |
| L.19 | signify 表す | L.22 | take the place of 取って代わる |
| L.24 | itemize 箇条書きにする | L.24 | paginate ページ数字を付ける |
| L.25 | attachment 付属物 | L.25 | the Statue of Liberty 自由の女神 |
| L.25 | tablet 平板 | L.26 | the US Declaration of Independence 米国の独立宣言 |
| L.27 | note 注目する | L.28 | publication 出版 |

***Grammar Points***

助動詞 should ／理由 as ／比較級の協調 much

## Unit 9　Visiting Boston

***Reading Section***

***Vocabulary Focus***

| | | | |
|---|---|---|---|
| L.2 | Puritan 清教徒 | L.3 | the American Revolution アメリカ独立戦争 |
| L.4 | Boston Tea Party ボストン茶会事件 | L.5 | prestigious 一流の |
| L.5 | residence 住宅 | | |
| L.5-6 | Ralph Waldo Emerson (1803- 1882) ラルフ・ワルド・エマーソン　米国の作家 | | |
| L.6 | Louisa May Alcott (1832- 1888) ルイーザ・メイ・オルコット　米国の作家 | | |
| L.6 | outskirts 郊外 | L.10 | get around 見てまわる |
| L.11 | hop-on hop-off trolley ホップオンホップオフ・トローリー（途中で乗ったり降りたりできる観光用バス） | | |
| L.12 | duck boat ダック・ボート　水陸両用バス | L.14 | option 選択 |
| L.16 | Abraham Lincon (1809-1865) エイブラハム・リンカン　米国第 16 代大統領 | | |
| L.16-17 | the Emancipation Proclamation 奴隷解放宣言 | L.18 | enslave 奴隷にする |
| L.19 | slavery 奴隷であること | L.21 | fugitive 逃亡者 |
| L.22 | walkway 通路 | | |

***Grammar Points***

無生物主語／ for ~ to ...（不定詞の意味上の主語）／再帰代名詞 themselves

## Unit 10 Jazz

***Reading Section***

***Vocabulary Focus***

| | | | |
|---|---|---|---|
| L.1 | genre ジャンル | L.2 | originate 生まれる |
| L.3 | street corner 街角 | L.6 | distinctive 際立った |
| L.6 | term 専門用語 | L.7 | characterize 特徴づける |
| L.8 | standard track number ミュージシャンに繰り返し演奏される名曲 | | |
| L.9 | enchant うっとりさせる | L.9 | deliberately 故意に |
| L.10 | metrical accent 韻律のアクセント | L.11 | ensemble アンサンブル |
| L.12 | bass guitar ベースギター | L.15 | complement よく合う |
| L.17 | stimulate 刺激する | L.17 | awaken 目覚めさせる |
| L.18 | pleasure center 快楽中枢 | L.18 | invoke 呼び起こす |
| L.19 | jazz piece ジャズの曲 | L.19 | alleviate 緩和する |
| L.19 | depression 憂うつ | L.21 | ambient music 環境音楽 |
| L.23 | talented 才能ある | L.23 | improvise 即興演奏する |
| L.23 | riff ジャズで反復楽節に合わせて変奏する | L.24 | replicate 繰り返す |

***Grammar Points***

may ＋ have ＋過去分詞／前置詞＋関係代名詞／命令文＋ and

## Unit 11 Mercy Killing

***Reading Section***

***Vocabulary Focus***

| | | | |
|---|---|---|---|
| L.3 | depressed 落ち込んで | L.6 | razor かみそり |
| L.6 | insert 差し込む | L.8 | highlight 強調する |
| L.8 | unveil 明らかにする | L.8 | underlying 潜在している |
| L.8 | euthanasia 安楽死 | L.10 | mercy killing 安楽死 |
| L.13 | incurable 不治の | L.14 | suspicion 容疑 |
| L.15 | lethal 致死量の | L.15 | dose 薬の一服 |
| L.16 | natural death 自然死 | L.17 | tolerate 許容する |
| L.17 | blog ブログ | L.17 | illegal 非合法の |
| L.17-18 | no matter how much ~ どんなに～しようとも | L.19 | ethical 倫理上の |
| L.21 | living will リビング・ウィル（生前遺言） | L.21 | regarding ～に関して |
| L.22-23 | take ~ into consideration ～を考慮する | L.24 | dignity 尊厳 |

***Grammar Points***

過去完了形 had ＋過去分詞／ not A but B ／ no matter ＋疑問詞

## Unit 12 Online Communication

***Reading Section***

***Vocabulary Focus***

| | | | |
|---|---|---|---|
| L.1 | virtual ネットワーク上の | L.1 | emergence 出現 |
| L.2 | be used to ~ing 慣れる | L.2 | text message メールする |
| L.4 | take on （それまでと異なる様相を）帯び始める | L.5 | be forced to 強制的に～する |
| L.6 | thrust （ある状態に）押し込む | L.7 | web-cam ウェブカメラ |
| L.8 | engaging 魅力的な | L.9 | isolation 孤立 |
| L.10 | messenger 情報を伝える人 | | |
| L.12 | communicator コミュニケーター , コミュニケーションをとる人 | | |
| L.12 | take steps 行動を起こす | L.15 | ensure 確実にする |
| L.20 | non-verbal 言葉を用いない | L.21 | presenter 司会者 |
| L.22-23 | facial expression 顔の表情 | | |
| L.25 | platform プラットフォーム（コンピュータの基盤となるシステム） | | |

***Grammar Points***

人を表す those ／動名詞主語／使役動詞 let

## Unit 13　The Secret of Rosetta Stone

***Reading Section***
***Vocabulary Focus***

| | | | | | |
|---|---|---|---|---|---|
| L.1 | construction　建設 | L.1 | Fort Julian　ジュリアン砦 | L.2 | purely　全くの |
| L.2 | by accident　偶然に | L.2-3 | stick out　突き出る | L.5 | hieroglyphics　象形文字 |
| L.5 | demotic　民衆文字 | L.6 | assume　推定する | L.7 | inscription　碑文 |
| L.8 | script　文字 | L.8 | decode　解読する | L.9 | portion　部分 |
| L.11 | the Nile valley　ナイル川流域 | L.12 | piece　継ぎ合わせる | L.12 | sudoku　数独 |
| L.12 | game of *go*　囲碁 | L.13 | get stuck　行き詰まる | | |
| L.13 | frustrate　欲求不満を起こさせる | | | L.13 | wrong move　間違える |
| L.14 | go around in circles　堂々巡りする | | | L.16 | breakthrough　打開 |
| L.16 | decipher　解読する | L.17 | linguist　言語学者 | L.17 | well-versed　精通した |
| L.17 | Coptic　コプト語 | L.19 | unlock　解き明かす | L.19 | code　象形文字 |
| L.21 | reference　参照文献 | L.25 | Egyptian section　エジプト室 | | |
| L.25 | the British Museum　大英博物館 | | | L.26 | artifiact　人工遺物 |

***Grammar Points***

of ＋抽象名詞／ It is assumed that ／強調構文

## Unit 14　Neuvola

***Reading Section***
***Vocabulary Focus***

| | | | | | |
|---|---|---|---|---|---|
| L.1 | pregnancy　妊娠 | L.3 | suffix　接尾辞 | L.5 | maternal　妊婦の |
| L.5 | mortality rate　死亡率 | L.6 | distribute　分配する | L.6 | sterilize　殺菌する |
| L.9 | midwife　助産師 | L.9 | initiative　主導権 | L.9 | check-up　健康診断 |
| L.10 | nutrition　栄養 | L.10 | hygiene　衛生 | L.10 | expectant mother　妊婦 |
| L.10-11 | childcare package　子育てセット | | | L.12 | institutionalize　制度化する |
| L.12 | municipality　自治体 | L.15 | assign　割り当てる | L.15 | health nurse　保健師 |
| L.17 | counseling　カウンセリング | L.19 | hospital fee　入院費 | L.19 | free of charge　無料 |
| L.20 | regardless of　にかかわらず | L.20 | nationality　国籍 | L.21 | subsidize　助成する |
| L.21 | day-care service　保育所 | L.21 | irrespective　無関係の | L.22 | accessible　利用しやすい |
| L.25 | comprehensive　包括的な | L.27 | kindergarten　幼稚園 | | |

***Grammar Points***

While …ing ／分詞構文 having ＋過去分詞／ every/each ＋単数名詞

## Unit 15　COVID-19

***Reading Section***
***Vocabulary Focus***

| | | | | | |
|---|---|---|---|---|---|
| L.1 | onset　始まり | L.1 | utter　全くの | L.1 | chaos　混沌 |
| L.3 | infection　感染 | L.4 | mutated strain　突然変異した株 | L.5 | overwhelm　あふれる |
| L.6 | invisible　目に見えない | L.8 | fatal　致命的な | L.8 | contagious　感染力のある |
| L.8 | detect　見つける | L.9 | exhibit symptoms　症状がでる | L.9 | carrier　感染源 |
| L.11 | pharmaceutical　製薬の | L.12 | vaccine　ワクチン | L.12 | revolutionary　革命的な |
| L.13 | Pfizer　ファイザー社 | L.13 | Moderna　モデルナ社 | L.14 | complication　合併症 |
| L.15-16 | immunization program<br>集団予防接種 | L.16 | impractical　実行できない | L.20 | virtual　仮想の |
| L.22 | sanitary habits　衛生習慣 | L.24 | blessing　幸福 | | |
| L.24-25 | take for granted　当たり前のことと思う | | | L.26 | strike　考える |

***Grammar Points***

付帯状況 with ／ SVOC ／部分否定

MEMO

**MEMO**

MEMO

# MEMO

**Amazing Future Prospects** —Exploring Human Activity—　[B-965]
グローバル社会に生きる —聞く、読む、書く力を鍛える—

1刷　2024年2月26日

| | | |
|---|---|---|
| 著　者 | 伊與田 洋之 | Hiroyuki Iyoda |
| | 赤塚 麻里 | Mari Akatsuka |
| | 土居 峻 | Schun Doi |
| | マリキットG.マナラング | Marikit G. Manalang |
| | 室 淳子 | Junko Muro |

発行者　南雲　一範　Kazunori Nagumo
発行所　株式会社　南雲堂
〒162-0801　東京都新宿区山吹町361
NAN'UN-DO Co., Ltd.
361 Yamabuki-cho, Shinjuku-ku, Tokyo 162-0801, Japan
振替口座 : 00160-0-46863
TEL:　03-3268-2311(営業部:学校関係)
　　　03-3268-2384(営業部:書店関係)
　　　03-3268-2387(編集部)
FAX:　03-3269-2486

編集者　田中　仁／中西　史子
組　版　柴崎　利恵
装　丁　奥定　泰之
検　印　省　略
コード　ISBN978-4-523-17965-8　C0082

Printed in Japan

E-mail : nanundo@post.email.ne.jp
URL : https://www.nanun-do.co.jp/